The 7 Rivers Civilization

The 7 Rivers Civilization

The 7 Rivers Civilization

The 7 Rivers Civilization

MIXTE
Papier issu de sources responsables
Paper from responsible sources
FSC® C105338

# The 7 Rivers Civilization

The 7 Rivers Civilization

© 2025 HERVÉ LE BÉVILLON
ÉDITION : BOD - BOOKS ON DEMAND, 31 AVENUE SAINT-RÉMY, 57600 FORBACH, BOD@BOD.FR
IMPRESSION : LIBRI PLUREOS GMBH, FRIEDENSALLEE 273, 22763 HAMBURG (ALLEMAGNE)
ISBN : 978-2-3226-1408-0
DÉPÔT LÉGAL : MAI 2025

# The 7 Rivers Civilization

*Sapta Sindhu: the Rig Veda civilization*

Herve Le Bevillon

The 7 Rivers Civilization

All illustrations whose origin is not cited come from wikimedia commons:
https://creativecommons.org/licenses/by-sa/4.0/

# The 7 Rivers Civilization

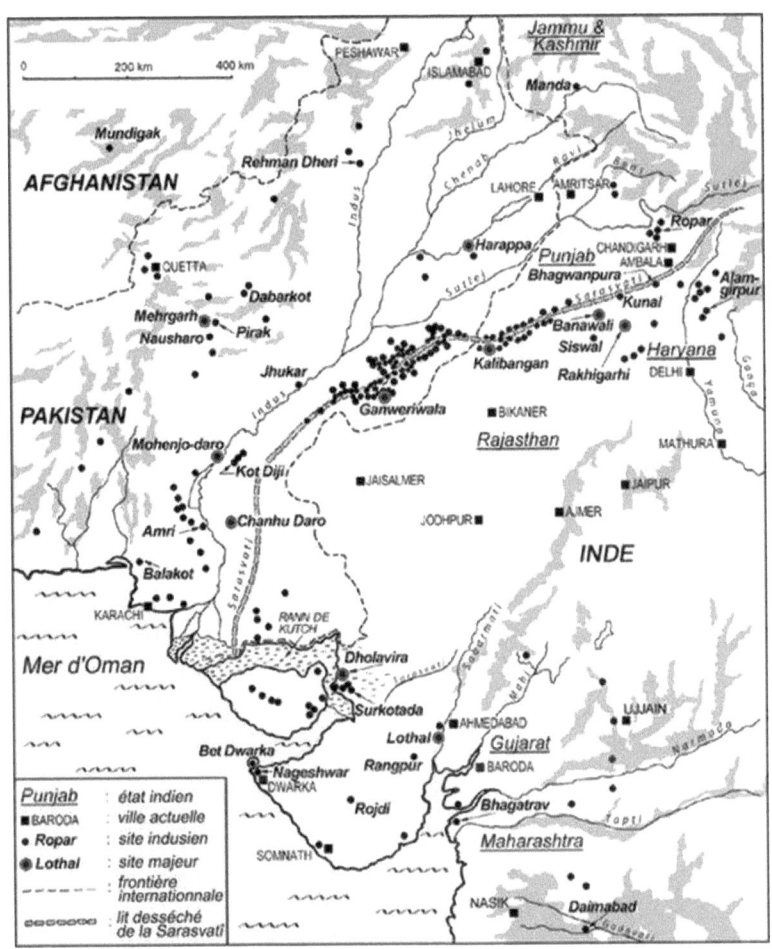

*Michel Danino Map: L'Inde ou l'invasion de nulle part.*
*Les Belles Lettres. 2006*

The 7 Rivers Civilization

By the same author

The Rig Veda, New & complete translation in English

7 years on the road

Website: https://rigveda.blog/

# FOREWORD

In January 2018, I started the translation of the Rig Veda. I had heard about it and read several books about it, including "The Secret of the Veda" by Sri Aurobindo.

By chance, one evening, some time before, while zapping on my television, I had come across a documentary on Arte[1]. It presented, very succinctly, the so-called Indus civilization which had moved me deeply.

This documentary took me back forty-five years, when I went to India, like thousands of young Westerners. I had gone there after five years of hitchhiking around the world, penniless, including three years in Africa.

My goal in coming to India was not to find a guru or to seek any spiritual liberation, that was already done.

In 1970, after I had been on the road for over two years, I had this spiritual experience that cannot be described or properly named.

So I went to India to live the life of a sâdhu, a renunciate. That is what I did for almost a year. I lived with them the life of a naga-baba, a category of sâdhus who go almost naked, covered in ashes, from temple to temple[2], owning only what they can carry. I never spoke of the Veda with them, but the life I led made me understand many things..

I am not an intellectual. I hated school and dropped out in the second year of high school[3]. I took a vocational certificate as a projectionist and worked in a cinema in

---
[1] Franco-German television channel.
[2] Or from dhuni to dhuni.
[3] In year 11 in the english system

Brittany for six months, plus two more in a post-synchronization studio in Paris, before setting off on the road in 1967 with my last paycheck.

So I did not follow the classic path of Sanskrit or ancient civilizations enthusiasts. Of course, my readings had made me discover their point of view and their first-degree interpretation of the Rig Veda.
There is still no book in French on the so-called Indus civilization. The rare newspaper articles that talk about it give information that dates from the middle of the 20th century.

I couldn't really understand why Western archaeologists and specialists in ancient civilizations especially didn't want to hear about the Rig Veda, which tells of events taking place in the same place and, for some of them, at the same time.

The arguments put forward were: "It's religion, we don't understand anything about it", "The Rig Veda dates from 1500 BCE, with the arrival of the Aryans, so later", And when, during my discussions with those who support this vision of things and I asked them for references, on what they based this assertion, they answered me: "it's a scientific consensus" or "it has already been widely demonstrated". I was even sub jected to insults.
So, I decided to translate it, into French and English, to see what it was really like.

Once my translation was finished and published, I realized that my introduction was a bit too short to explain the context in which these hymns were composed. Here is the result of the analysis I made of it by deciphering its metaphors and taking into ac count the archaeological discoveries found in books in English, since there is nothing available in French, and hours of conferences on the web, still in English, on this sub ject.

*** 

Like all civilizations, it includes two aspects that we will see one after the other: the material and the spiritual.

**The material** : not being an archaeologist, I simply summarized what I discovered in my many readings, notably those of JM Kenoyer, BB Lal, Michel Danino... and the many videos found on the web. I illustrated this part with royalty-free photos, which I transformed into black and white.

If you can afford it, I recommend the excellent book by Johnathan Marc Kenoyer "The ancient cities of the Indus Valley civilization" Oxford University Press Pakistan. He is the one who has excavated Mohenjo-Daro the most. This book is magnificently documented, with superb photos.

**The spiritual** : here, it is simpler. After having learned Sanskrit, without the intention of speaking it correctly one day[1], but simply to translate, I devoted all my time to this translation. Reading Sri Aurobindo's book: "The Secret of the Veda" greatly helped me to decipher the metaphors.

Of course, I could be wrong in the interpretation of the Rig Veda and its connection with the so-called Indus civilization. Honestly, I have asked myself this question more than once.

I checked everything, controlled everything. Obviously, there are still points to clarify, both in the text of the Rig Veda and in the adequacy between the ruins and the old text. But I am still fundamentally convinced that the Rig Veda was indeed THE book, oral of course, of this civilization located between the Ganges and the Indus and which ended almost 4000 years ago.

To keep informed, go to my website:
https://rigveda.blog

---

[1] No one is required to do the impossible. Sanskrit, especially Vedic, is very difficult to pronounce correctly for a Westerner.

The 7 Rivers Civilization

# Table of contents

FOREWORD..................................................................................11
The material..................................................................................19
Architecture and Artifacts............................................................23
    The cities...............................................................................24
    Objects of everyday life........................................................34
    The economy.........................................................................35
    Trading posts in Iran and Sumer...........................................41
    The ports................................................................................41
    Mysterious writing.................................................................43
    Weapons.................................................................................47
    Social and political organization:..........................................47
    Burials....................................................................................50
    Clothing and adornments......................................................51
    Musical instruments..............................................................53
    Games and leisure.................................................................53
    Weights and measures..........................................................54
Historical......................................................................................57
The spiritual.................................................................................59
    Spirituality.............................................................................63
    The sacrifice:.........................................................................63
    The private sacrifice:.............................................................64
    Public sacrifices:...................................................................65
    The Mantra............................................................................66
    Techniques for achieving enlightenment..............................68
    The three worlds:..................................................................69
    Mâyâ :....................................................................................70
    Rishi :....................................................................................71
    Reincarnation :......................................................................71
    The moral :............................................................................71
    Lineage, descendants:...........................................................71

- Lexicon...................................................................................73
- The Rig Veda.............................................................................75
- Where and when?......................................................................81
  - Geography...............................................................................83
  - Dates........................................................................................85
  - When did it end?.....................................................................92
- The great myths........................................................................97
  - Vritra.......................................................................................97
  - Shushna...................................................................................99
  - Shambara...............................................................................102
  - The Dasyus (or Dâsas)..........................................................103
  - The War of the Ten Kings.....................................................107
  - Other wars between Âryas....................................................111
  - Spirituality............................................................................113
    - The sacrifice.........................................................................113
  - The soma...............................................................................117
    - Religion or Pure Spirituality................................................125
    - The goal to be achieved for each.........................................125
    - The three worlds..................................................................126
  - How the society works..........................................................127
  - The place of women..............................................................129
  - Manners................................................................................131
    - The funeral...........................................................................131
    - Sexuality..............................................................................132
    - Alcohol:...............................................................................136
    - Meat:....................................................................................137
    - The Eunuchs........................................................................138
    - Material Wealth...................................................................138
    - The sâdhus...........................................................................138
  - Drought and soma shortage...................................................141
  - The tenth mandala.................................................................145
  - Concrete functioning of the society.....................................155
    - The castes............................................................................155

The opposition and its arguments..................................................159
    The horses..........................................................................159
    Linguistic...........................................................................161
    Genetics.............................................................................163
    ...........................................................................................168
    After 1900 BCE..................................................................169
    Politics...............................................................................171
Proposal of a history..................................................................173
    Conclusion.........................................................................177
        Today's world................................................................178
        The end of civilizations..................................................181
        So, is it over?................................................................186
    Bibliography......................................................................189

The 7 Rivers Civilization

# The material

I suggest you study what I call the 7 Rivers Civilization. You have certainly heard of it under other names such as the Indus Civilization, Harappan Civilization, Indus-Sarasvatî Civilization, or simply Sarasvatî Civilization.

This civilization was located in northwest India, covering present-day Pakistan, from the Ganges to the Indus, and from northern Afghanistan to southern Gujarat.

I call it this to distance myself from political recuperation from all sides, and to bring a little serenity to understand this magnificent civilization almost totally unknown in France.

The Seven Rivers Civilization, in its urban phase, emerged about 5,500 years ago, at about the same time as Egypt and Mesopotamia. At the same time, other smaller civilizations flourished in a region stretching from northern Afghanistan, to Turkmenistan, and Iran: the Oasis Civilization, in the Karakum Desert, and the Oxus Civilization in Afghanistan and Tajikistan. City-states, such as Merhgarh, already existed at this time and probably served as a model for these new civilizations.

These small civilizations were the heirs of local shamanism and were characterized by their pacifism. Some of them were even led by women, which was far from common at the time.
These civilizations excelled in agriculture, animal husbandry and crafts. They shared a common spirituality and practiced almost similar rituals.

Of course, these civilizations traded with each other and maintained extensive cultural and social exchanges. The Indian and Iranian civilizations, in particular, had the same main gods and spoke very similar languages.

Gradually, these civilizations evolved and expanded to give rise to large, prosperous cities. In the space of about two thousand years, the Seven Rivers Civilization developed to reach an impressive extent, equivalent to more than twice the size of France. It was of an importance comparable to Egypt and Mesopotamia combined. It thus marked history with its planning, its quality of life, and its intelligence.

Thus, this study will allow us to delve into the history of one of the most important and influential civilizations of Antiquity which leaves archaeologists almost speechless.

*Mohenjo Daro*

The 7 Rivers Civilization

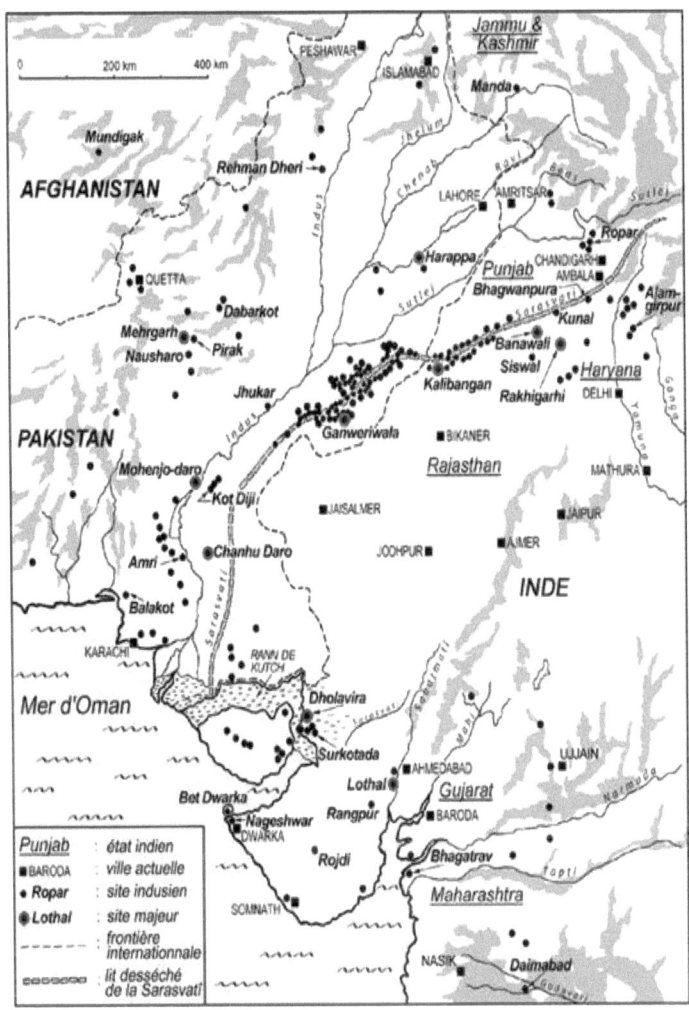

Map by Michel Danino: "India or the invasion from nowhere".
Ed. Les belles lettres. 2006

The 7 Rivers Civilization

# Architecture and Artifacts

The first cities of the Seven Rivers Civilization emerged about 5,500 years ago. It was initially a rural civilization. Over the centuries, it became urban, around 3,500 BCE[1]. It went through several stages of development. Around 2,700 BCE, a period called the Mature phase began. This era was characterized by a high population density for that time, as well as great prosperity.

At that time, it was one of the three most developed early civilizations. It covered an area twice the size of France, or more than a million square kilometers. It was as large as Egypt and Mesopotamia combined. It was the most populated civilization of its time. Over the centuries, while many small civilizations have disappeared, that of the Seven Rivers still exists, of course greatly modified by time and people. It left a lasting mark that contributed to the formation of the modern India we know today.

This West Asian region was rich in natural resources, which favored its economic and social growth. Trade with other civilizations of the time also played a key role in its development. Agriculture, crafts and urban planning allowed for significant exports throughout the region.
Archaeology shows us well-organized, planned, thoughtful cities with new infrastructures, sewerage systems to evacuate waste water and dwellings designed for the well-being of its inhabitants. As in other civilizations, cities were built along rivers. This is where its name *Sapta Sindhu* comes from, the seven rivers in Sanskrit.
These technological and social advances allowed this civilization to flourish for about a millennium and a half. Through its influence, it laid the foundations for many practices and customs that still persist in Indian culture today. For example, weights and measures are still the same, 4,000 years later, in everyday life and traditional practice.

---

[1] Before common era.

## The cities

Harappa, the first city of this civilization, was discovered in 1910 during work on the railway that the British were building in what is now Pakistan. The British needed ballast and noticed that the locals were helping themselves with bricks from a nearby hill. Intrigued, they went to take a closer look and discovered an ancient city in ruins, buried by time.

Ten years later, John Faithfull Fleet discovered Mohenjo-Daro, another site of this civilization. Since the architecture and weights and measures were the same, he concluded that it was indeed a civilization, and not independent city-states. Both cities were located on the Indus River, so it was called the Indus Civilization.
Excavations began at Mohenjo-Daro in 1927 under the direction of John Marshall. This work was continued by Mortimer Wheeler, who introduced an efficient method of excavation known by his name, also called: "Square excavation".

Like all his future colleagues, he unearthed a city built of baked bricks, erected on a brick platform and surrounded by walls also made of bricks, except in Gujarat, where stone replaced them, notably at Dholavira and Lothal.

At first, the walls were interpreted as military protection, similar to those of other ancient civilizations.
But archaeologists quickly concluded that these walls were actually intended to protect the city from floods from the Indus and other nearby rivers that overflowed in the summer.

For example, in Mohenjo-Daro, it was necessary to take a boat to move between the lower town and the upper town in summer, during the monsoon when the plain was flooded.

Subsequently, other important sites were discovered including Dholavira and Lothal in Gujarat, Rakhi Garhi, Kalibangan, Banawali, Ganweriwala on the dry Ghaggar river in India, called Hakra in Pakistan.

Quickly, the importance of this new civilization became evident. Its main charac teristics were unique for the time: there were no palaces, no temples, no armies, no slavery, no excessive wealth, no apparent poverty, no flagrant inequalities, no statues, no monuments like pyramids or ziggurats, and no glorification of the ego. No statues to the glory of this one or that one, no bas-reliefs depicting wars, prisoners being chained or put to death.

*Millions of fired bricks were used*

The urbanization of this civilization was intelligent and carefully planned. The cities were built in an orderly manner, with avenues running north-south and streets running east-west. Mohenjo-Daro is nicknamed the "Manhattan of prehis tory." It contrasted with the cities of other civilizations where everything usually converged towards a royal palace or a main temple.

This highlighted a communal and relatively egalitarian way of life without visi ble power structures, which is unique for a civilization. The discoveries amazed archaeologists who had never experienced this. It is, unfortunately, still unknown to the western public, in general. They are not interested in non-centralized civi lizations without monumental buildings, hanging gardens and other pyramids.

*"The Indus civilization represents a very perfect adjustment of human life to a specific environment which can only result from years of patient trials and accumulated experiences."*
Marshall, John. *Mohenjo-daro and the Indus Civilization: An Official Account of the Archaeological Excavations at Mohenjo-daro Carried Out by the Government of India Between the Years 1922 and 1927.* Arthur Probsthain, 1931.

*Harappa excavations 1925*

The houses, even those of the most modest inhabitants, had remarkable facilities for the time, such as toilets and a system of protection against humidity. Each house had an interior courtyard around which the rooms were organized. Life at this latitude takes place outdoors. It was therefore very practical.

Even the houses of the poor were equipped with a bathroom and a sewage system, an innovation unknown elsewhere at that time. Unlike other civilizations, even the simplest dwellings had these facilities. Archaeologists have unearthed dry toilets in every house. They have also found a few flush toilets, which did not exist anywhere else at that time. It also seems that there were public toilets at Mohenjo-Daro. Not all archaeologists agree on this.

The houses of wealthy families were certainly distinguished from those of poor families, but this difference was mainly due to the presence of additional rooms. Some houses, those of the more affluent, even had one or two additional floors.

*The brick columns are actually wells.*

The interior design also varied between rich and poor. The difference was probably seen in the interior equipment: carpets, furniture, dishes...

What is certain is that all the dwellings, whether modest or not, were designed in the interest of their inhabitants by ensuring their comfort and well-being, whatever their social status.

Water management in this civilization was a priority. The infrastructure put in place to ensure the supply of drinking water was efficient. A wastewater drainage system allowed it to be evacuated outside the city limits, thus avoiding any contamination of drinking water.

In regions such as Mesopotamia and Egypt, where potable and non-potable waters were more or less mixed, people had to drink beer, to avoid diseases related to poor water quality, such as dysentery and cholera.

Numerous wells, some reaching a depth of 30 meters, were present at every crossroads and even in some houses. These wells were lined with trapezoidal bricks, which gave them exceptional solidity.

In large cities, the common areas were located in a place that 19th-century archaeologists called "the citadel." This is a word they got from their studies of Greek or Roman civilizations. It was a part of the city that was raised by large embankments and surrounded by walls. In the citadel, there was a large common room without a roof where the inhabitants could gather for various activities, plus what archaeologists called a community granary.

At Mohenjo-Daro there was also a large bath. This bath, in the shape of a pool, was built so that people could perform ablutions. There were small rooms around the bath and stairs to go down into the water.

This large bath was probably used for purification rituals.

# The 7 Rivers Civilization

*The common areas of Monhenjo Daro: the large bath.*

Altars with one or more hearths were discovered at Lothal and Kalibangan by B. B. Lal, later director of the Archaeological Survey of India.

The first cities emerged around 3,500 BCE, but long before that, large villages had been existing since at least 6,000 BCE. These villages were the earliest forms of social organization in the region that we have records of.

In Rakhi Garhi, for example, before the town was built, houses were cylindrical holes dug in the ground, with a roof placed over them.

This transition from large villages to early cities marks an important step in the evolution of society and urbanization in the Indus-Ghaggar Valley. Building techniques evolved from simple buried structures to more modern houses. Here is an example of ingenuity: in some houses, archaeologists have found clay balls studded with pieces of charcoal. They were buried under the floor of the house, to absorb moisture.

Archaeology has found no evidence of violence at the sites of this civilization, regardless of the location and level excavated. All researchers agree that it was completely peaceful. There is no representation of warriors in the artifacts or sculptures of this period. Furthermore, the bones of the corpses found in the cemeteries do not show any injuries indicating combat or deliberate violence. There is no evidence of arson in the remains of the buildings, and no arrowheads have been found planted in the walls.

The excavations also did not reveal any objects related to war, such as helmets or shields. Weapons, made of copper, were found, but there is no evidence that they were weapons of war. This lack of evidence of conflict or violence suggests that the inhabitants of this civilization lived in a very peaceful society, focused on trade, agriculture and community life rather than war. This pacifism is a remarkable characteristic of this civilization, especially when compared to other cultures of the same time that had strong military traditions. The conclusions of archaeologists and researchers on this point are unanimous: it was a harmonious, peaceful and stable society.

With an estimated population of around five million, which was enormous for the time, the Seven Rivers Civilization was comparable to those of Egypt and Mesopotamia combined.
The structure of the cities of this ancient civilization reveals a well-developed so cial organization and community life. The cities were generally divided into two or three distinct parts: the lower city, the upper city and the citadel[1].

The lower city housed several residential and commercial districts, where artifacts have been found, showing us that life was communal. The jewelry and stat uettes discovered suggest a form of communitarianism among the population.

Were these cultural, professional, or linguistic communities? The question is still being debated by historians and archaeologists. Archaeological evidence suggests some cultural diversity and trade with other regions, but the language(s) spoken by the inhabitants remains a subject of research and de bate. In this geographic area, dozens of different languages are still spoken today. It is likely that this was the case at that time.

---

[1] It seems that not all cities had a citadel.

*Mohenjo Daro*

The Seven Rivers Civilization reached its peak before declining around 1,900 BCE, with the notable exception of the Gujarat region, which continued to thrive for about another five centuries. Several factors contributed to the demise of this flourishing civilization. Among the main reasons, there was a major climatic disruption that occurred around 2,200 BCE. This disruption manifested itself in a period of drought that, according to various studies, could have lasted from ten years to a century, which is enormous. This drought would have affected water resources and agriculture without decreasing harvests. Indeed, no signs of a decline in exports have been revealed in Mesopotamia.

In addition, the region has been hit by a series of earthquakes, which has amplified the difficulties already posed by the climate.

These seismic tremors, very frequent in the Himalayas, had a disastrous effect on the Sarasvatî, the main river of the Seven Rivers Civilization, which is known today as Ghaggar in India and Hakra in Pakistan.

# The 7 Rivers Civilization

*Monhenjo Daro*

The earthquakes contributed to the drying up of this river, causing the majority of the population to flee to the Indus Valley, as they could no longer live there. However, the cities of the Indus Valley, which were already very populated, were quickly overwhelmed. The evacuation of practically the entire population was therefore decided, mainly to the Ganges Valley. It seems to have taken place without violence or destruction.

## The 7 Rivers Civilization

Climate change combined with natural disasters have therefore precipitated the decline and disappearance of this society, which is totally unique in all of human history.

*"The Ghaggar-Hakra River, which flows through the northwestern regions of India and Pakistan, is often identified by some scholars as the mythical Sarasvatî River mentioned in ancient Hindu texts. This identification is based on hydrological and archaeological evidence, which suggests that the Ghaggar-Hakra was once a perennial river, corresponding to the description of the Sarasvatî in the Vedas."*
Oldham, C. F. (1893). *"The Sarasvatî and the Lost River of the Indian Desert."* The Journal of the Royal Asiatic Society of Great Britain and Ireland, pp. 49-76.

Contrary to what is written in the photo, it is not a goddess.

*"Recent research in geoarchaeology and satellite imagery has supported the hypothesis that the Ghaggar-Hakra River may be the ancient Sarasvatî. Analyses show dried-up riverbeds and changes in watercourses that are consistent with Vedic descriptions of the Sarasvatî as a mighty river that gradually dried up."*
Yash Pal et al. (1980). Remote Sensing of the 'Lost' Sarasvatî River. Proceedings of the Indian Academy of Sciences (Earth and Planetary Sciences), 89(3), pp. 317-331.

*"The Ghaggar-Hakra is often associated with the Sarasvatî because of geographical and linguistic similarities. Many sites of the Indus Valley Civilization

*are located along its ancient course, suggesting that this river played a central role in the lives of the inhabitants, much like the Sarasvatî in ancient texts."* Danino, Michel (2010). *The Lost River: On the Trail of the Sarasvatî.* Penguin Books India.

## Objects of everyday life

In addition to the many beautiful pieces of pottery that are masterfully crafted, archaeologists have discovered thousands of artifacts of all kinds . They have found a lot of jewelry, especially necklaces made with precious stones such as lapis lazuli, as well as gold, copper, and carnelian. There were also bracelets finely carved from shells. They have also unearthed many children's toys. They have found the ancestors of chess sets as well as dice.

***

## The economy

The 7 Rivers Civilization, was based on agriculture, livestock breeding and crafts, like all the first civilizations in History. Agriculture was a vital component of this ancient society because it allowed to feed the ever-growing population, and to export food surpluses to Mesopotamia, the Arabian Peninsula, Bahrain and Iran, by sea, and the small civilizations in the north of the country.

The Seven Rivers Civilization also practiced animal husbandry, particularly of cattle, sheep, goats and other small domestic animals.

At the same time, crafts occupied an important place in society, with artisans specializing in pottery, metalworking and weaving.

*Harappa Museum*

The area in question, arid today, was lush green at the time. Plenty of sunshine and plenty of water from the Himalayas ensured bountiful harvests, especially since they practiced grid-type cultivation. That is, one type of crop was sown lengthwise, and another type was sown widthwise, depending on their need for sunshine.

Until 2,200 BCE, the date of the great drought, they cultivated wheat, barley, lentils, chickpeas, vegetables of all kinds and fruits.

After the great drought, they developed the cultivation of millet[1] and rice. They compensated for the rainfall deficit with good irrigation and great agricultural di versity, to be able to face the significant climatic hazards.

Trade quickly developed, not only with smaller civilizations such as those of the Karakum Desert and the Oxus, but also with Mesopotamia, Bahrain and the Ara bian Peninsula.

The Seven Rivers Civilization was a peaceful, trading society that exported far more than it imported.

The main products exported by the 7 Rivers Civilization included:
- Agricultural products: Wheat, barley, lentils, vegetables of all kinds.

---

[1] The current Indian state is redeveloping millet cultivation due to climate change.

- Textiles: The inhabitants wove cotton, which was probably exported in the form of sheets.
- Handicrafts: Manufactured products such as pottery, beads, carnelian jewelry and other precious stones.

*Pipeline*

- Metallurgical products: Copper and bronze objects.
- Seafood: Products such as shells, to make jewelry, especially bracelets, and fish were exported to the interior regions.

Mesopotamia was a major market for carnelian beads and other luxury items during the Seven Rivers Civilization. Sumerian cuneiform tablets mention Meluhha, which was the name of this civilization, indicating commercial transactions. Archaeological evidence suggests the existence of Indus merchant colonies in Mesopotamia.

" *The discovery of Indus seals in Mesopotamia and Mesopotamian-style seals in the Indus Valley provides compelling evidence of long-distance trade between*

*these two ancient civilizations. The presence of Indus artifacts in Mesopotamian cities such as Ur and Kish indicates a well-established network of trade and cultural exchange."*
Possehl, Gregory L. _Indus Age: The Beginnings_. University of Pennsylvania Press, 1999, p. 245.

*"Artifacts such as carnelian beads, ivory objects, and specific types of pottery found in Mesopotamian archaeological sites strongly suggest that there was significant trade between the Indus Valley and Mesopotamian civilizations. These objects, often found in elite tombs, imply that they were highly valued and traded goods."*
Kenoyer, Jonathan Mark. Ancient Cities of the Indus Valley Civilization_. Oxford University Press, 1998, p. 187.

*"The presence of Indus weights and measures in Mesopotamian sites, as well as references to Meluhha (supposed to be the Indus region) in Mesopotamian texts, provide clear evidence of a sophisticated trading system. This system facilitated the exchange of goods such as textiles, timber, and precious stones, highlighting the economic and cultural interactions between the two regions."*
McIntosh, Jane R. The Ancient Indus Valley: New Perspectives. ABC-CLIO, 2008, p. 220.

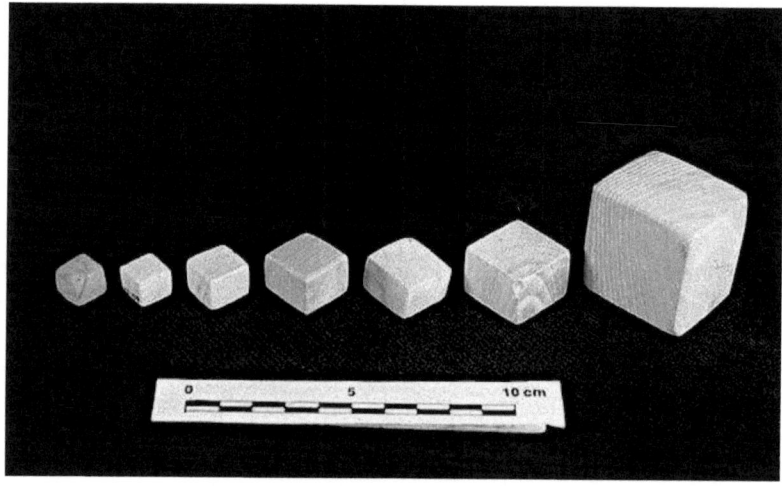

Despite their significant exports, merchants and artisans also imported goods that were not available locally:
- Precious metals: Gold and silver, used for the manufacture of jewelry and other luxury items.
- Gemstones: Lapis lazuli and other gemstones from areas of present-day Afghanistan and beyond.
- Exotic products: Objects made of ivory, certain types of wood and other exotic materials.

Exports were made by land, caravans and sea. In front of each large city, caravanserais welcomed merchants from all sides. The entrance gates to the cities were a cart wide. This meant that a toll was required to enter the city.

Navigation was the safest and fastest way to travel long distances.
The shipments were accompanied by finely engraved seals in their handwriting that no one has been able to decipher, which could probably indicate the seller and/or the shipment.

*Harappa*

# Trading posts in Iran and Sumer

The Seven Rivers Civilization's trade extended as far as Iran and Mesopotamia, and perhaps even further west. Some scholars have mentioned Egypt, but solid evidence is lacking.

### 1 - Counters in Iran

Trade relations with Iran (Elam and other regions) were well established. Trading posts in this region served as transit points for goods en route to Mesopotamia and other western regions. These posts facilitated:
- Storage and distribution of goods: The products were stored there before being shipped further west.
- Local exchanges: The counters also served as exchange points with local populations, allowing direct transactions.

### 2 - Counters in Sumer

Trade relations between the Seven Rivers Civilization and Sumer were particularly important, as shown by archaeological finds of seals in Mesopotamia.

# The ports

All rivers flow into the sea or the ocean. The Sarasvatî and the Indus are no exception. There must have been ports for both the Indus and the Sarasvatî.

Underwater archaeology has discovered a wall under the sea in Bet-Dwarka, in Gujarat, which could well be the remains of a quay. Unfortunately, it has not been really studied. We will know more in a few years.

On the other hand, in Lothal, still in Gujarat, the remains of what archaeologists have called a port are still clearly visible.

But, there is a doubt, because this port, or loading dock, is anything but practical. Even sheltered by a jetty leading to a lighthouse, a port always overlooks the sea. They are never in the middle of the land.

According to the Breton sailors I asked, it would rather be a "fishery", that is to say a fish trap. This fish trap is ideal for storing them: they remain alive, within reach and are easy to catch.

Another explanation was given to me, again by Breton sailors: it would rather be a shipyard. This explanation is even more credible than the fishery.

*The "port" of Lothal today*

Below is a reconstruction of the *"port"* of Lothal in full activity. And the hypothesis of a shipyard does not seem at all absurd, but on the contrary, very credible.

The 7 Rivers Civilization

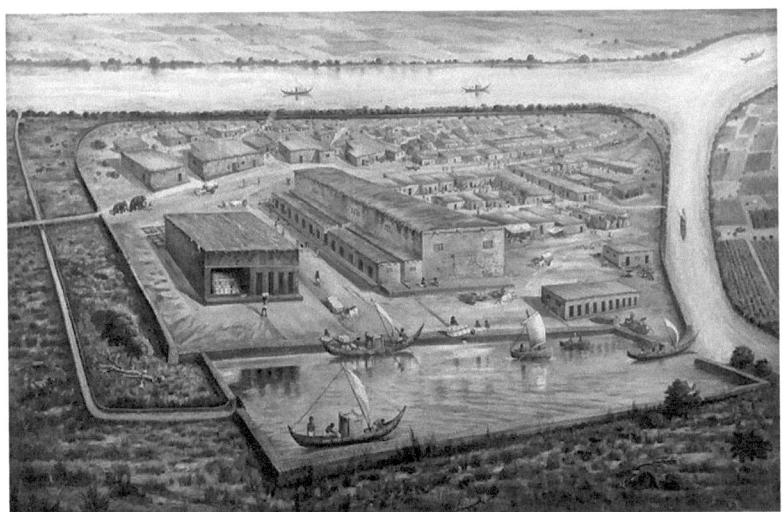

*The practical side of the "port" is not immediately obvious to Breton sailors.*

# Mysterious writing

Steatite seals, discovered in various regions, including abroad, such as Bahrain and Mesopotamia, reveal the existence of close commercial and economic links between the Seven Rivers Civilization and other cultures of the time. These seals, made of steatite, a soft rock that is easy to carve, were often decorated with very fine designs.

*Unicorn, animal composed of three animals: bull for the body, horse for the head and antelope for the horn.*

The 7 Rivers Civilization

The inscriptions on these steatite seals remain undecipherable to this day, and this is not for lack of trying.
These thousands of seals discovered in various regions show us the importance of commercial and cultural exchanges between the 7 Rivers Civilization and its neighbors.

Many interpretations of this writing have been formulated. Here are some of them:

- Rekha Rao's: She proposed that the Indus script may have been a system of notation used primarily for religious purposes. The seals, worn around the neck, may have been memory aids for apprentice priests. She also suggests that many symbols in the Indus script may represent plants and trees, and that they were used in the context of Vedic sacrifices[1].

- That of Asko Parpola who is a leading scholar of the Seven Rivers script. He concluded that the script could be an early form of the Dravidian language. He compared it with modern and ancient Dravidian languages and proposed that the script could represent place names, people, and religious titles[2].

- That of Iravatham Mahadevan who also supported the Dravidian hypothesis and considered that the script of the 7 Rivers would be a proto-Dravidian script. He used data from the Brahmi script - the alphabet that preceded the Devanagarî - and from the Dravidian languages to suggest phonetic values for certain symbols[3].

[1] Rao, Rekha. "The Symbolism on the Indus Seals." (2009).
[2] Parpola, Asko. "Deciphering the Indus Script." Cambridge University Press, 1994.
[3] Mahadevan, Iravatham. "The Dravidian Proof of the Indus Script via the Brahmi Writing." Harvard Oriental Series, 1970.

The 7 Rivers Civilization

- That of SR Rao who proposed that the Seven Rivers script was alphasyllabic and could be read from right to left. He tried to relate some symbols to the letters of the Brahmi alphabet, suggesting a continuity between the two writing systems[1].

- Walter Fairservis proposed that the Seven Rivers script might be a form of logo graphic proto-writing, in which each symbol represented a word or idea. He attempted to decipher the symbols based on their archaeological and cultural contexts[2].

Several types of supports for this writing existed, including representations of yogis in the Baddha konasana posture. This posture is particularly difficult to hold. You have to be an experienced yogi to be able to do it.

---

[1] Rao, S.R. "Lothal and the Indus Civilization." Asia Publishing House, 1973
[2] Fairservis, Walter A. "The Harappan Civilization and Its Writing: A Model for the Decipherment of the Indus Script." Oxford & IBH Publishing, 1992.

Other characters are represented, including the famous Pashupati. The master of animals.
According to Indian researchers, it represents the god Shiva.

# Weapons

Despite the complete lack of evidence indicating the existence of an army, weapons have been discovered at the site. These include arrowheads, spears, axes and knives, the majority of which were made of copper.

While copper blades are aesthetically pleasing, they are far from effective as weapons of war. In comparison, a stone war axe would be far more useful and durable than its copper counterpart.

The presence of these copper weapons could indicate that their manufacture dates back to a period before the Bronze Age.
This period is often associated with a non-urban phase, when societies were still essentially rural. The weapons found from this period seem to be more ceremonial weapons than weapons of war.

They, especially arrows, could also be used for hunting. Bones of wild animals have been found during excavations of several sites. The inhabitants were not vegetarians.

# Social and political organization:

Obviously, the absence of structures such as palaces or temples, as well as the ab sence of armies and slavery, suggests that this civilization operated on different principles than other great civilizations of the time, and even our contemporary societies. There was no glorification of the individual ego or apparent misery. This indicates that the functioning of this society was neither centralized nor ver tical.

This civilization had opted for a decentralized and horizontal social organization, probably based on collective decisions and a relatively equal distribution of responsibilities and resources. Instead of having a central authority or rigid social classes, everyone could play a role within the community.

These characteristics clearly distinguish it from modern societies, which are often marked by rigid hierarchical structures, centralized power centers, and pronounced socio-economic inequalities. Based on the available evidence, it is quite possible to see this ancient civilization as an alternative model where authority was soft and shared.

This non-authoritarian and relatively egalitarian organization allows for reflections on the potential of societies operating without the domination and hierarchies that frequently characterize our current systems.

*"Archaeological evidence suggests that the Indus civilization was characterized by a relatively egalitarian social structure, with no clear evidence of a centralized state or ruling elite, but that it was also not governed by a rigid hierarchical system."*
Kenoyer, Jonathan Mark. Ancient Cities of the Indus Valley Civilization. Oxford University Press, 1998.

*"The absence of palaces, large temples or large tombs in the Indus Valley suggests that power and wealth were not concentrated in the hands of a few. Instead, governance may have been carried out by local councils or assemblies, indicating a decentralized but cooperative societal structure."*
Possehl, Gregory L. "The Indus Civilization: A Contemporary Perspective." Rowman Altamira, 2002

*"The Indus civilization appears to have functioned through a series of autonomous, interconnected urban centers rather than through a single, centralized state. This decentralized system facilitated cooperation and mutual support among the different city-states."*
Wright, Rita P. "The Ancient Indus: Urbanism, Economy, and Society." Cambridge University Press, 2010.

The functioning of the Civilization of the 7 Rivers was based on community and consensual principles, favoring cooperation and participation of the whole society. Contrary to authoritarian and brutal models, this society seems to have favored collective decision-making and managing business in a concerted manner.

This functioning suggests that the leaders of the Seven Rivers Civilization were not characterized by an oversized ego or an authoritarian exercise of power. On the contrary, the absence of oversized egos among the leaders of ancient Indian society would have favored a climate of dialogue and consensus within the community.

This form of governance suggests a certain form of democracy in the 7 Rivers Civilization. Participatory decision-making and the valuing of the group over the individual seem to have been fundamental characteristics of this ancient society. It was a social organization totally different from any we know. The lack of ego of the leaders was most likely the reason. Here is what some famous people think about it:

*"The ego often disrupts our relationships and creates conflict because it causes us to prioritize our own needs and desires over those of others, leading to a lack of empathy and understanding."*
Dalai Lama. *The Art of Happiness: A Handbook for Living.* Riverhead Books, 1998.

*"The moment the ego arises, it brings a sense of separation, a sense of 'me' versus 'the other.' This fragmentation leads to conflict, discord and suffering in society."*
Tolle, Eckhart. *"A New Earth: Awakening to Your Life's Purpose."* Penguin Group, 2005.

*"Ego creates division and prevents us from seeing our interconnectedness with others. When ego dominates, it fuels misunderstanding, prejudice and social discord."*
Thich Nhat Hanh. *"The Art of Living: Peace and Freedom in the Here and Now."* HarperOne, 2017.

The urban societies of our time are ruled by individuals with inflated egos and authoritarian power. Dictatorships, where power is concentrated in the hands of a single individual or a small group, perfectly illustrate this reality. Even in some regimes that claim to be democratic, free elections are influenced by a ruling class that has no desire to lose its power. This leads to inequalities and manipulation of public opinion, particularly by its media, which relay many lies.

In this context, the predominance of ego and personal interests within political elites compromises the proper functioning of democratic institutions and the representativeness of governments. Decisions taken are motivated by personal ambitions rather than by the general interest, which leads to abuses and injustices.

It is therefore essential to promote transparent governance, based on accountability, fairness and citizen participation, to ensure democratic functioning. The balance between individual and collective interests is essential to ensure fair and balanced governance, responding to the needs and aspirations of the whole society.

# Burials

Funeral practices within the 7 Rivers Civilization were both burial and cremation according to the funeral customs of the different communities of the time.

Burial was the most common practice. The dead were buried with a few personal objects or offerings. However, cremation was also practiced, depending on the community and the region concerned.

*"The majority of Harappan burials are of the elongated type, where the body is laid out lengthwise. Evidence for cremation as a method of disposing of corpses is scarce but does exist."*
Kenoyer, Jonathan Mark. "Ancient Cities of the Indus Valley Civilization." Oxford University Press, 1998.

*"The principal mode of burial of the dead was inhumation, although various methods such as lying, split and urn burials were practiced."* Wheeler, Mortimer.
*"The Indus Civilization."* Cambridge University Press, 1968.

Archaeological discoveries have revealed an aspect of society that is quite contrary to what was done in the other two great civilizations: the absence of luxurious and ostentatious tombs overflowing with treasures. On the contrary, the tombs that have been unearthed are simple and without excess of wealth.

Unlike the other two civilizations, Egypt and Mesopotamia, where royal or noble tombs were filled with rich offerings and treasures, the burials of the Seven Rivers Civilization were discovered without grave goods. Some jewelry and personal items were found, but without the opulence and pomp associated with the other two great civilizations of the time.

This simplicity of burials perhaps reflects a form of social equality within this society, where inequalities of wealth and status were not as marked as in other civilizations.

## Clothing and adornments

The statuettes show us that men and women went bare-chested, like sub-Saharan African women a few decades ago, without it bothering anyone.

They wore many necklaces and bracelets, both men and women. These jewels were often colorful and made of natural materials (Lapis Lazuli, carnelian, gold etc.).

In addition to jewelry, hairstyles were also very important. They were very elaborate and probably distinguished different regional, linguistic or other communities. Each group had its own style.

*One of the most remarkable features of the Indus civilization terracotta figurines is the variety and detail of the clothing depicted. Women often wear long, pleated skirts, while men are depicted with loincloths or dhotis.*
Possehl, Gregory L. *The Indus Civilization: A Contemporary Perspective*, AltaMira Press, 2002.

*"The hairstyles of female figurines from the Indus civilization reveal a wide variety of styles, including elaborate updos and braids. Some figurines even wear hair jewelry, such as headbands or hairpins."* Kenoyer, Jonathan Mark. *Ancient Cities of the Indus Valley Civilization*, Oxford University Press, 1998.

*"Male Indus figurines are often depicted with ornaments such as necklaces and bracelets, suggesting that personal adornment was important to the inhabitants of this civilization."* Wheeler, Mortimer. *Civilization of the Indus Valley and Beyond*, Thames & Hudson, 1966.

Among the statuettes found, only one is relatively large[1]. It represents a naked dancer, wearing bracelets on the upper part of her left arm. .

---
[1] 14 cm.

## Musical instruments

In the ruins of ancient cities, several musical instruments were found. Among the finds was a flute with seven holes. It allows to create more harmonious melodies than a flute with six holes.
They also had a nine-stringed instrument that resembles a modern harp. A kind of metal kettledrum was also found.

Other stringed instruments have also been discovered. Some of them were bowed, as for the Sarods, or plucked, as for the Sitars.

## Games and leisure

Children played with various types of toys: animal figurines, utensils to imitate the daily tasks of adults. Carts were also common. They were equipped with wheels that turned.

Among the animal figurines, the bull was the most widespread. It was often used in Indus Valley seals and in many artifacts. The bull symbolized strength and fertility. We will return to this later.

Animal figurines, utensil sets, puzzle games and carts were toys found in almost every home.

***

## Weights and measures

From Dholavira in Gujarat to Shortugai in northern Afghanistan, from the Ganges to the Indus the weights and measures were the same:

Weights: These were usually made of stone and cubic in shape, and the smallest was the equivalent of a sesame seed.

Units of length: These were transmitted using rules engraved in ivory or bone, divided into equal units. The divisions were 33.5 mm, or 1.32 inches.

# The 7 Rivers Civilization

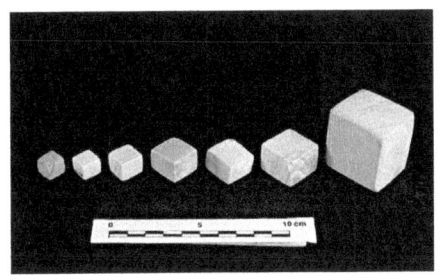

**Harappa**

## Historical

Archaeologists have classified the different periods of civilization as follows, using the term Harappan:

1- Pre-Harappan – 7,000 to 5,500 BCE : This period is well represented by the city-state of Mehrgarh, which knew and mastered agriculture, livestock breeding, and crafts. Mehrgarh exported copper about 6,000 years ago.

2 - Early Harappan – 5,500 to 2,800 BCE : Seals found in Egypt, Bahrain, and Mesopotamia show that international trade was already well established. An important port, perhaps that of Sarasvatî, must have been at Bet-Dwarka in Gujarat.

3 - Mature Harappan - from 2,800 to 1,900 BCE : The cities that already existed, are transformed from this date and adopt new measures for the bricks: 1x2x4, instead of 1x2x3. New cities appear. At the end of civilization, there were about 1,000 cities, spread throughout the territory.

4 - Late Harappan - from 1,900 to 1,500 BCE : Decline of civilization following a climatic disturbance, including the famous drought of 2,200 BCE, and the drying up of the Sarasvatî which must have dealt it a final blow.

The population living on its banks, the majority, moved to the banks of the Indus, which caused an overpopulation incompatible with climate change. It is also possible that unrest in Mesopotamia, their largest economic partner, weakened foreign trade. But no trace of voluntary degradation, characterizing a violent end, has been found.

5 - Post-Harappan - from 1,500 to 600 BCE : The cities were abandoned, and people moved towards the south and the Ganges plain, for the majority of them, but also towards Iran and therefore towards Anatolia and to the North, for those who lived in Afghanistan, towards what is today Tajikistan and Uzbekistan.

# The spiritual

There is no civilization that can function without some form of spirituality. It is the cement of society. Without it, concerns are only material and mercantile, and its end is inevitable.
We have seen that the Seven Rivers Civilization did not have a temple. However, does this mean that it had no spirituality?

\*\*\*

At the same time, between about 4,000 BCE and 1,900 BCE, and in the same place, between the Ganges and the Indus, other events of considerable importance were taking place: the events that are recounted in the Rig Veda.

This monument of literature is totally ignored by archaeologists and other Western researchers working on the 7 Rivers Civilization. And yet, its metaphors provide us with a lot of information.

There are several reasons for this refusal to study it:

1- The belief in an Aryan invasion or migration, which would have taken place in 1,500 BCE. A people of undetermined origin, but white, would have arrived on the banks of the Sarasvatî and would have brought Sanskrit, the gods and religion to the wild Indians. According to them, this invasion-migration would be described in the Rig Veda.
This theory is that of Max Müller, one of the first translators of the Rig Veda.

*"The Vedic hymns form the backdrop to the Aryan invasion of India, a movement that occurred around 1500 BC. The Aryan conquerors brought with them their language and their social structure which then evolved into the system we know today as the caste system."*
Max Müller, History of Ancient Sanskrit Literature , London, 1860

He was followed by all other Western Indianists of that time and even now by most of them.

*"The Aryans, a nomadic people, invaded the Indian subcontinent around 1500 BC, overtaking the indigenous Harappan civilization and ushering in a period of significant cultural and linguistic transition."*
R. E. M. Wheeler, The Indus Civilization , Cambridge University Press, 1953

*"The Rigveda reflects a migratory event, led by Aryan tribes, who entered the Indian peninsula around 1500 BC, an event that reshaped the entire cultural and social framework of the region."*
Hermann Oldenberg, Die Religion des Veda , Berlin, 1894.

2 – The unbearable questioning of a supposition, which became a fact at the beginning of the 19th century: the date of this invasion-migration. It had been set, at the very beginning of his translation, by Max Müller at 1,200 BCE , but he aged it by three centuries, for some reason or other[1], to 1,500 BCE. The impressive Indian literature must have something to do with it.
This date, unanimously adopted by Western scholars, has become the basis of a number of studies in scientific fields ranging from linguistics to anthropology and even genetics.

*"The theory of an Aryan migration to the Indian subcontinent around 1500 BCE is supported by linguistic, archaeological, and textual evidence. Although there is debate about the nature and extent of this migration, the date itself remains widely accepted among scholars."*
Thapar, R. Early India: From the Origins to AD 1300, University of California Press, 2002.

*"The influx of Indo-Aryan speakers into the Indian subcontinent around 1500 BCE is a well-established fact based on comparative linguistics and correlated archaeological findings. This period marks a significant cultural and linguistic transformation in the region."*
Witzel, M. The Origins of the World's Mythologies, Oxford University Press, 2012.

---

[1] Let us not forget that the general Christian belief fixed the creation of the Earth at 4000 years BCE.

*"The arrival of the Aryans in South Asia around 1500 BCE is the cornerstone of our understanding of the ancient history of the region. This date is supported by a convergence of evidence from various fields of study, including textual analysis of the Rigveda and material culture.*
*Parpola, A. The Roots of Hinduism: The Early Aryans and the Indus Civilization, Oxford University Press, 2015.*

Contrary to what is announced in these quotes, there is no archaeological trace of this migration. And it is not for lack of having looked. But, let us leave these certainties for the moment, and look more closely at the spirituality that is more or less hidden behind these war metaphors.

*The main gods are often called bulls*

# Spirituality

As everyone knows, the Rig Veda is the basis of all Indian spirituality, whether it is Hinduism, Buddhism or Jainism. And this reason appears through metaphors, which should be deciphered.

But first, let's try to clarify some concepts.

The whole life of this civilization revolved around sacrifices. The typical sacrifice[1], the Agnistoma, – the praise of fire, of Light, of Enlightenment – took place every year in the spring, at least. All the Masters of the House, that is to say all the rich families, who therefore have power, and consequently, all the leaders of the society participated. They had to drink the soma at least once a year, during the full moons of spring.

# The sacrifice:

In monotheistic religions, it is mandatory to have faith, to believe in a god, other wise, you are not really human, and you will roast in hell for eternity.

The monotheistic god has a human-like mind, with its qualities and defects. Among these, we find jealousy, wickedness, authoritarianism and even cruelty.

To avoid this, the faithful must obey its laws, otherwise he will roast in hell. These laws were brought by preachers, as we can still find in any market in North African countries, or the Middle East.

If we look more closely at how things happened in the Bible, we can say that it is not the prophet himself who dictates the laws or writes them, but faithful follow ers who knew the prophet...

---

[1] Available in different ways depending on needs.

Which is to say that these laws were, purely and simply, written by men. Generally by the leaders of these religions.

These laws are, in fact, laws of the same type as our current laws, dating of course from another era, but it is the same principle: laws for living in community.

In the Rig Veda, up to the ninth mandala, we are far from all that. There is no di vine law, but a law specific to the Âryas: to offer sacrifices and therefore, to drink soma to obtain enlightenment. That's all! And then, everyone knows what they must do, how they must live. Their experience will have made them understand it.
In the tenth mandala, we will see some very specific moral lessons appear. But we will come back to them.

Sacrifice is the mass of Vedic times. At that time, yoga already existed (see the seals found at Mohenjo-daro and elsewhere), even if this word does not exist to designate a specific discipline in the Rig Veda[1], ascetics, sâdhus, already existed too[2]. Sacrifice, as we can imagine it, was therefore the "official" ceremony. That of the Masters of the House, that is to say of the " bourgeois" of the time.

It was an occasion to ask the gods for material goods or fusion with the Brahman, depending on the sacrifice desired. The whole life of civilization revolved around it. It had considerable importance.

In reality there were two types of ceremonies, public and private sacrifices.

## The private sacrifice:

It is a family ritual that people did at home, as Indians continue to do today. It consisted of mantras with a ritual in which a little clarified butter was given to the gods by pouring a spoonful into the fire. This rite still exists, it is now called a puja. The head of the family did it alone or he hired one or more priests. There could be consumption of soma.

---

[1] The hymns are full of terms like union, harness, etc.
[2] RV 10.136

## Public sacrifices:

Public sacrifices were the occasion for great festivals overflowing with color, music and great rejoicing with snake charmers, musicians, dancers, etc. When we know the Maha Khumba-Melâ where millions of pilgrims gather in Allahabad every twelve years, we can easily imagine what it must have been like 4000 years ago. Indian spirituality is absolutely not sad.

1 – The sacrifice offered by the "Masters of the House" to obtain something: children, goods... These sacrifices could last from one day to one year. They swallowed up to an entire year of the sacrificer's income[1]. A sheep, a goat, a billy goat, a bull and even, for special occasions, a horse were strangled[2].

2 – The sacrifice for the Brahman. This is the most sacred of the two, and it is the one that is in the second reading of the hymns. It is in this sacrifice that the soma is drunk. All the Masters of the House had to offer at least one each year, during one of the full moons of spring.

Gods are external and internal. When we call upon a god to ask for spiritual riches or immortality, we are calling upon our own inner forces. Gods are symbols. Man and nature are not separate. The forces that govern the Universe are the same as those that govern Man.

## The Enlightenment :

The basis of Indian spirituality, whatever the religion, is "Enlightenment[3]" which Hindus today call Moksha[4], but which we can also call Truth , Revelation , Mys-

---

[1] The person who offers the sacrifice.
[2] This technique allows them to say that the animal does not protest during the sacrifice.
[3] This term is used in the West, but is very restrictive, but for lack of a better one, it is the one I will use.
[4] Deliverance.

tical Ecstasy, Seeing God[1], etc. There is no right word. It is the awareness of Brahman[2], the Absolute, Nirvana, the Holy Grail...

*"Brahman is the universal principle of all that exists. It is both immanent and transcendent, and it transcends all duality. As such, it is both the One and the Many, Being and Non-Being, All and Nothing ."*
Aldous Huxley (The Perennial Philosophy)

*"Brahman is the ultimate reality, the immanent essence of the universe that underlies and transcends all forms of manifestation. It is beyond words and thoughts, for it is the absolute unconditioned by time, space or causality."*
Ananda K. Coomaraswamy ( The Dance of Shiva ).

*"Brahman is the supreme reality of the universe, the eternal and infinite cosmic soul that permeates everything. It is the central enigma of existence, both the impalpable presence and the source of all that is manifest, thus unifying the visible and the invisible."*
Heinrich Zimmer ( Philosophies of India ).

In the Indian tradition, even today, beyond the daily problems, that is all that matters. All paths to get there are good. No judgment is made on those that are chosen.

# The Mantra

Mantra is not a formula that one recites to please a god, but it is a technique that allows one to produce spiritual energy.
A mantra is composed of three equally important elements: the text, the sound, the rhythm.

**The text:**
The verses of the Rig Veda were used separately from others during the sacrifice. And each has a spiritual meaning, which can be supplemented by a clue regarding the history or life of that civilization.

---
[1] Although this expression induces a duality.
[2] The Concept of the Absolute in the Upanishads. Surendranath Dasgupta.

The rishi who composes it uses past events that become metaphors. For example, when Indra is asked to give strength and kill enemies, it is about spiritual strength, spiritual energy. Today's Indians call it by different names depending on the current they follow: kundalini, shakti are the most common.

Killing enemies means getting rid of everything that prevents us from reaching the Light: selfishness, greed, hypocrisy, dishonesty, gratuitous violence and all the negativity that binds us to this earthly life.

**The sound:**
The rishis attached great importance to the sound the shloka gives when recited. For example, the first verse of the first hymn of the first mandala:

agnimīḷe purohitaṃ yajñasya devaṃ ṛtvījam | hotāraṃ ratnadhātamam ||

Here, the am sound, which is the accusative declension of almost all words after the verb, is pronounced in a certain way, with the aim of vibrating the seventh chakra, at the very top of your head. You can feel it when you pronounce this mantra by concentrating on this region of your head.
Now, these shlokas are meant to be learned by heart so that they can be passed on to others, down through the ages. For this to work well, it is essential that this mantra be easy to remember.
If in the construction of the sentence, there was no word suitable for the desired sound and rhythm of the shloka, the rishi himself created the word he wanted from the root. And if the declension was not right, it did not matter much. The ultra-rigid rules of classical Sanskrit were far from being fixed, since they would only appear 1,500 years later.

**The rhythm:**
This is about metrics. I had never heard this word before translating the Rig Veda. It is a very learned word to say the number of feet per sentence. For example, this first verse is a gayatri meter: three times 8 feet:

agnimīḷe purohitaṃ/ yajñasya devaṃ ṛtvījam/ hotāraṃ ratnadhātamam.
Here too, sometimes the rishi had to compose a word for the occasion. Which is why the Rig Veda is full of words that are found only once in the entire history of Sanskrit.

The mantra, well pronounced, concentrating on the meaning and on the chakra, combined with controlled breathing, allows the functioning of the pineal gland, connected to the 6th and 7th chakras as explained in the teaching of the tantric yoga:

*"Where the mind is concentrated, there resides energy. By the repetition of sacred mantras, one can awaken the inner energy which is linked to the Ajna center, located between the eyebrows, governing clairvoyance and intuition[1]."*
*"Psalmody (a vocal technique of reciting a text on a single note) sends vibrations to the crystal palate, activating in particular the pineal gland and the hypothalamus. You can chant a mantra such as OM (Aum) or the song of HU for example*

## Techniques for achieving enlightenment.

There are many of them. Since man has existed, he has developed many diverse and varied techniques. Whether it is the sound of the drum that puts you into a trance, yoga, meditation, pranayama[3], bhakti[4] or the consumption of plants containing a molecule from the tryptamine family[5], there is bound to be something that suits you.

In the Rig Veda they use soma. The mysterious plant which is an entheogenic plant[6]. The ninth mandala is entirely dedicated to it. It is the only mandala which is solely dedicated to one god.
In all his descriptions, there is never any mention of leaves, seeds, fruits or flowers, but of fibers[7].

And then in 2009, Russian archaeologists found a tapestry in a tomb in Mongolia dating from the first century AD, woven in Palestine or Syria, and embroidered in the cities of the Indus.

---

[1] Excerpt from traditional tantric teaching.
[2] Craniosacral Chi Kung by Mantak Chia and Joyce Thom.
[3] Breath control .
[4] Worship.
[5] DMT: The Spirit Molecule. Exergue Editions. 2017.
[6] Who places the divine in man.
[7] Amshu.

The motif depicts priests of Zoroastrianism, a daughter of Vedism, the Iranian religion, venerating a mushroom that they identified as an Indian variety of psilocybe cubensis[1], that is, a mushroom that contains psilocybin.

Now Zoroastrianism used the same drink (haoma) as Vedism[2]. They therefore deduced that soma also contained it. Which corresponds entirely to the descriptions in the hymns of the Rig Veda and to the description of the ninth mandala.

And then we have a shloka that tells us a little more:

*1.100. 16 – Red and brown horses, like the soma plant, with the spot on the forehead, celestial, which bring the riches of Rjrashva, with a magnificent chariot drawn by vigorous horses go towards the house of Humanity[3].*

But, we will come back to that....

## The three worlds:

For the Vedic people, there are three worlds: Heaven, Earth and the Intermediate World.
- Heaven is Brahman, Ecstasy, the Absolute. Non - Duality .
- The Earth This is our ordinary world as we perceive it in a normal state of consciousness.
- The Intermediate World, this is where the gods, the demons, the spirits, the celestial nymphs, the humans on their way to mystical ecstasy are. This is where all the paranormal events occur. But, despite the very impressive experiences, we remain in duality, even if we can get very close to the goal .

This principle of division into three is found everywhere:

- The three gunas , - set of qualities - which create the world: sattva - all that is pure and luminous.
rajas - energy, action -

---

[1] https://fr.wikipedia.org/wiki/Psilocybe
[2] https://scfh.ru/en/news/we-drank-soma-we-became-immortal-/
[3] This shloka gives the impression that it is describing a fly agaric instead.

tamas - inertia, degradation.

These gunas combine to give matter and spirit. The Indians say that matter is solidified spirit.
- The trimurti which will be born a few centuries later:
    - Brahma[1] the creator,
    - Vishnu who maintains and operates,
    - Shiva who destroys.
- The three conditions for successfully knowing Brahman:
    - pure dispositions of mind;
    - a suitable environment;
    - a means used that is effective.
- The definition of Brahman itself, sat-cit-ananda[2].
- The three components of the mantra.
- The three doshas in Ayurvedic medicine, and in almost everything if you look carefully etc.

## Mâyâ :

Mâyâ, which is generally translated as illusion, is the perception that our senses give us of the world around us. Reality is Brahman, everything else is only Mâyâ. Our eyes cannot see everything (infrared, ultraviolet, atoms, protons, neutrons, etc.) Our ears cannot hear everything (infrasound, ultrasound, etc.). The same goes for our understanding. We can only understand Reality (Brahman) if our in

tellect, and therefore our ego, is silent[3]. Mâyâ is therefore a vision of the world at a certain level, but absolutely not reality.

---

[1] The deified Brahman.
[2] Being – Consciousness – Bliss.
[3] Which is almost impossible for a Western intellectual to understand.

## Rishi :

Rishi is usually translated as seer, sage or poet. They are the authors of hymns. Some of them were the Purohita[1] of a king[2]. Some of these are very well known for having played a role in the foundation myths like Divodâsa and his grandson Sudâsa.

## Reincarnation :

This notion exists in the Rig Veda only in the tenth mandala, with one or two exceptions, at a time when the soma had probably disappeared. But, on the other hand, there is much talk there of immortality.

This word, immortality, appears 86 times in the entire Rig Veda. We find it 15 times in the first mandala, 1 time in the second, 13 times in the third, 5 times in the fourth, 11 times in the fifth, 10 times in the sixth, 4 times in the seventh, 3 times in the eighth, 6 times in the ninth, and 17 times in the tenth.
Needless to say, this is not about physical immortality, as some Western Indianists of the 19th century believed.

## The moral :

The Rig Veda doesn't give no moral lessons, and only in the tenth mandala, and even then, with delicacy. It is up to each of us to find how to live in harmony with the universe, and therefore with others.

## Lineage, descendants:

A sacrificer can ask to have a large number of descendants, but this is not the case for ascetics, yogis, sâdhus and other renunciants, who are chaste. Even today, some brotherhoods of sâdhus as well as tantric teachings are done through lineages of an ancient rishi[3]. From master to student, not from father to son. From mistress to student, in the case of Tantrism[4].

---

[1] The equivalent of the chaplains of nobles in the West.
[2] This word comes from a root meaning to govern, represent, manage, administer.
[3] Whose name the disciple adopts.
[4] Theoretically.

# Lexicon

To decipher the metaphors, here is a small glossary. Do not hesitate to come back to it.

| | |
|---|---|
| Ambassador: | another name for Agni. Agni transmits the offering made to him to the other gods. |
| Aryaman: | the protective god of the Aryas. |
| Assembly: | the various people attending the sacrifice. |
| Asura: | spiritual being, in rivalry with the gods. |
| To grow: | to progress towards Brahman. |
| Dawn, dawn: | Enlightenment |
| Beauty: | the Brahman. |
| Clarified butter: | offering, symbol of Light. |
| Happiness: | the Brahman. |
| Loot: | spiritual riches, Enlightenment. |
| Cave: | where the Light is locked away. Mental blocks. |
| Chariot: | quick-wittedness |
| Horse: | strength, energy |
| Combat, battles: | internal struggles |
| Knowledge: | when one has had the experience of Brahman |
| Demons: | that which prevents enlightenment. |
| Waters: | symbol of purification. |
| Enemies: | ignorance, thoughts, actions that prevent enlightenment. |
| Son, child: | the positive results of the spiritual quest. |
| Waves: | the waves of Light, Enlightenment |
| Lightning: | Indra's weapon that kills ignorance to make way for Light. |
| Heroes: | Generally, those who have experienced enlightenment, but also gods. |
| Men: | human beings in general |
| Indu: | soma drops. Another name for soma. |
| intoxication: | the intoxication caused by tryptamine. Nothing to do with alcoholic intoxication. |

| | |
|---|---|
| Maghavan: | another name for Indra "the generous". |
| Manu: | the father of humanity, humanity. |
| Honey: | soma. the sweet. |
| Worlds: | the three worlds: Heaven, the intermediate world, Earth. |
| Food: | spiritual foods, soma. |
| Night: | ignorance. |
| Darkness: | ignorance, that which prevents enlightenment. |
| Ocean: | Vastness of the Mind |
| Word: | The mantra that brings enlightenment. |
| Strongholds: | anything that is contrary to enlightenment. |
| Abundance: | spiritual riches. |
| Portion, part: | the dose of soma poured into the cup. Part of spiritual wealth. |
| Rule: | The order of things. The cosmic order. The dharma. |
| Rich: | who is spiritually rich. |
| Wealth: | spiritual wealth, enlightenment |
| River: | flow of speech, of Enlightenment. |
| Savitri: | the Sun in its role as instigator, awakener. |
| Serpent: | Vritra, darkness, gloom. |
| Darkness: | ignorance. |
| Treasure: | the Brahman. |
| Union, to unite: | union with the Brahman |
| Cow: | Light |
| Truth: | Brahman. |
| Victory | the enlightenment. |

# The Rig Veda

It is the oldest book in the world. It has been passed down orally from generation to generation for at least four millennia, and continues to be so today in the same way.
It contains 1028 hymns, or songs of praise, addressed to gods or goddesses, but also to rivers, trees, mountains, generosity...

It is divided into ten chapters called mandalas. The first and last each contain 191 hymns. The others have different lengths.
Which gives us 191-43-62-58-87-75-104-103-114-191 hymns, for a total of 10,552 verses or shlokas.

These numbers, of course, have a meaning. The compilation was not done randomly. Unfortunately I have not found any convincing explanations.

The hymns are written by rishis. Rishis are wise poets belonging to several peoples united in the same spirituality. The mandalas 2-3-4-5-6-7 are called "the family books" because they are written by rishis who have succeeded one another over time, from historical families.

A thorough study, carried out by Brahmins for centuries, even millennia, has made it possible to reconstruct their genealogies, in a set of analyses called the Anukramnîs[1]. It has been completed by the genealogies of the kings found in the Puranas[2].
The oldest mandalas are the "family books". The first mandala is composed of hymns from several eras. The eighth and ninth are from a more recent era. The tenth was added much later.

---

[1] Clues.
[2] You will find all the details in: Rig Veda, an historical analysis by Shrikant G Talageri. Ed Aditya Prakashan.

All this has allowed to establish a chronology of mandalas: 6-3-7-4-2-5, for the oldest. The first mandala includes hymns from several ancient periods and some dating from the time of the eighth. Then come mandalas 8 and 9. These two mandalas are later, and most probably date back to the beginning of the urban period between 3500 BCE and 3000 BCE.

In the eighth we can already feel that spirituality becomes more "concrete" with hymn 8.48.3.1.

*We drank the soma. We became immortal. We entered the Light, we found the gods.*

The ninth, dating from all previous periods and composed by all families, is entirely devoted to Soma, the deified illuminating drink. It ended the penultimate compilation. As it was this one that concluded the Rig Veda, and as it is the only one to be devoted to one and the same god, we can assume that the soma had considerable importance in this society.
We will come back to this later.

The tenth was added much later[1]: some rishis come from unknown families and the vocabulary includes many words not found in any other mandala.

The historical families of rishis are descended from the first five peoples. Others will join them to, finally, constitute the India of today[2].

Here is the list of known rishi families:
Kanva – Angirasa – Agastya – Gritsamada – Vishvamitra – Atri – Vasishtha – Kashpaya – Bharata – Bhrigu.

The first five federations of peoples making up the Âryas[3] are as follows: Yadu – Turvasha – Druhyu – Anu – Pûru.

---

[1] However, since the Sarasvatî still flows abundantly, it must have been added before 1900 BCE.
[2] I'm not talking about the nation state that the British created in 1947.
[3] This word means Noble (in the noble sense of the term) and brings together those who practice the same spirituality which essentially consists of offering sacrifices and drinking soma.

Several kings are mentioned, but only two are of great importance, from a historical point of view: Divodâsa and his grandson Sudâsa. Both come from the main family, the one that will give its name to modern India: Bharata.

Divodâsa will fight the Dasyus, commanded by Shambara, and his grandson Sudâsa will win an internal war within the Âryas: the war of the ten kings. In all history that humanity remembers, this is the first war, with two battles, one on the Parushnî, the other on the Yamuna. The kings killed in this fratricidal war are mentioned in the 7th mandala.

The hymns, intended to be recited in sacrifices, are composed of metaphors based on events that occurred at different times, which can go back several centuries or even several millennia. They were not all composed at the time of the events recounted, but several centuries or even several millennia later,

The gods and goddesses represent nature, in its different aspects, but not only. We also find hymns to the union, to generosity, to rivers, to clouds...

Here are the main gods and goddesses[1]:

• **Aditi** : "unbound" She is the infinite, she is also the Mother of all things. She is the Mother Goddess[2].

• **Agni** : This is the sacred fire. It is also the messenger, because by pouring into the sacred fire an offering intended for a god, it is sent directly to him. But it is also the Light that comes to chase away the darkness. It is Enlightenment.

The **Angiras** : Angiras is the name of one of the first Rishis. Angiras are not necessarily gods, but they are sons of the gods and some gods are Angiras. They are found in the intermediate world, like the gods. They are the forces of Light. It is also the name of the family of this rishi.

The **Ashvins** : "Horse-like" They are twin gods, also called Angiras. They are the brothers of the Dawn. They are the sunrise, including in ourselves. Enlighten-

---

[1] Herbert, Jean (1980). The psychological interpretation of the Veda according to Shri Aurobindo. Philosophical Review of France and Abroad 170 (4):446-446.
[2] Or the feminine aspect of Brahman.

ment. They are called to heal the sick. They also represent two twin stars that appear before dawn: Castor and Pollux.

• **Indra** : "who is powerful" is the warrior god. He is also linked to the senses, and in particular to the intellect, which is a sense in India. He is the storm, his weapon is lightning. His power is revealed through the soma, which he loves. He conquers for man, wealth (the Brahman), the Cow (Light) and Horse(strength).

• The **Maruts** : "who cause death". They are the furious winds. They are the sons of Rudra, the companions of Indra. They are the gods of energy, power of will and vital force.

• **Mitra** : "friend". Inseparable and complementary to Varuna, he is the lord of love and friendship.

• **Rudra** : "the one who makes us cry". This is the first name of Shiva. He symbolizes destruction. He is violent and terrible while being compassionate towards all that suffers. He destroys darkness to make way for Light.

• **Sarasvatî** : "similar to a lake". It is the famous river, deified, where the first cities were located. It illuminates all meditations, it is the flow of the divine word which illuminates all thoughts.

• **Soma** : "which is pressed". It is the deified plant and its juice. It is the means of attaining enlightenment. The plant is pressed, the juice is mixed with water and milk. It was exchanged for a cow and, in the middle of the classical Vedic period, it cost the price of gold.

• **Sûrya** : "which shines". It is the Sun. It is the Light and the Truth. Its functions are luminous creation and luminous vision. It is Enlightenment.

• **Ushas** : "which illuminates". It is the dawn. It is also the Light of knowledge, it is Enlightenment, the Truth...

• **Varuna** : "that which surrounds". It is the ocean, the Sky. Companion of Mitra, it destroys all enemies. It is the conscious force of truth.

• **Vâyu** : " who blows". It is the deified wind, the breath. It is the master of the intermediate world. It is the master of life.

• **Vishnu** : " who is active". Guarantor of the functioning of the world, lord of activity, he helps man in his spiritual ascension.

• **Visvedevas** : These are all the gods.

# Where and when?

This is a question that divides both Indians and Westerners. The "official [1]"version tells us that the Rig Veda was composed by fierce "Aryan" warriors, speaking an Indo-European language, who came from Europe or the plains of Central Asia in 1,500 BCE, invaded India and brought Sanskrit, their gods and all their culture to the black-skinned Indians.

Since Nazism, this version has evolved slightly, and it is no longer a question of invasion but of migration from the plains of Ukraine. This soft, quasi-official version is based on the assertion that these events are recounted in the Rig Veda[2].

Well, let's take a closer look at that.

Of course we will find only a few solid pieces of evidence, no "smoking gun". So we will do as Justice does when it is in the same case: if we find enough serious and concordant clues, our inner conviction will be made.

---

[1] Of course, in History there is no official version, but there is always one that is considered the most probable.
[2] Oddly enough, with a few rare and very unlikely exceptions, no advocate of this migration-invasion can cite a single hymn or shloka that seriously confirms it.

The 7 Rivers Civilization

## Geography

What rivers are these? What are these seven rivers?

Well, these are the ones on which this civilization was born:
the Indus, the Jhelum, the Chenab, the Râvi, the Beas, the Sutlej, and the Ghaggar of their current names.
the Indus, the Vitâsta, the Askinî, the Parushnî, the Vipâsha, the Shutudrî, the Sarasvatî of their Vedic names.

The Vitâsta, the Askini, are tributaries of the Indus, as was the Shutudrî at the end of the Rig-Vedic period and which flowed into the Sarasvatî, like the Parushnî and the Vipâsha, before the earthquake which diverted its course.

Of course, over the centuries and millennia, civilization has spread, mainly to the West, but also in other directions.

Next, let us see the geographical location of the Rig Veda which is simply described in hymn 10.75, known in India as Nadi Shukta – the Hymn to the Rivers

*10.75.5 – Join in my praise, O Ganges, O Yamuna, O Sarasvatî [2], O Shutudrî [3], O Parushnî [4]. With the Asiknî [5], with the Marudvridha , with the Vitastata [6], listen with those who love the Soma in the cup.*

---

[1] Or the Hymn to the River or, to the Indus.
[2] Today: the Ghaggar in India and the Hakra in Pakistan.
[3] Today the Sutlej.
[4] Today: the Râvî.
[5] "the black one". A river, a tributary of the Indus.
[6] Tributary of the Indus, today the Jhelum.

1.75.6 – You are the first who comes together with the Susartu, the Rasâ, the Shvestya[1]. You come, O Indus, on the good chariot with those who come: the Kubha[2], the Gomatî[3], the Krumu[4], the Mehatnû[5]

There, it is simple and clear. Some rivers have kept their names: Ganges, Yamuna and Indus, the others have evolved over time and the arrivals of new populations that have taken place since that time and who spoke other languages.

Vedic Sanskrit was most likely a language of communication between different peoples who gradually united in Vedism. Perhaps it was that of the Pûrus, from whom the Bharatas came?

Of course, other hymns cite these rivers on the occasion of this or that exploit of one or more gods. Here are some examples:

*1.126.1 – With thought I bring these joyous hymns to Bhavya[6], dwelling along the Indus, for the unconquered king, desiring Glory, has squeezed from me a thousand soma juices.*

*4.30.11 – This chariot was lying and crushed in the Vipâsha[7], it went far away.*

*9.41.6 – O Soma, flow around us, in a protective flood, from all sides, flow like the Rasâ[8] in the Sky.*

A few places are mentioned. They have changed names since then, but one of them is still the same and gives us an interesting piece of information: Ghandara. It is a region between eastern Afghanistan and northwestern Pakistan, in the vicinity of Peshawar.

---

[1] Tributary rivers of the Indus.
[2] The Kabul River. Tributary of the Indus.
[3] "who has cows". Tributary of the Indus.
[4] Tributary of the Indus.
[5] Tributary of the Indus.
[6] "what should be."
[7] A river in Punjab flowing down from the Manali Valley.
[8] One of the Vedic rivers, tributary of the Indus.

*1.126.7 – (She speaks) I come very close to him, I touch him gently, Do you think my hair can disappoint him? I am Romasha, the sheep of Gandhara.*

So we can say that this civilization was located between the Ganges and the Indus, horizontally, and went at least as far as Gandhara, vertically[1].

So much for geography. Now, let's try to date the events that are told through these metaphors. There, obviously, it's less simple, but let's go anyway.

## Dates

To date an ancient period, which saw fighting, there are several elements that we can take into account, notably weapons and means of transport.

The first thing that jumps out at you: horse riding is not yet practiced. The oldest trace of horse riding dates back about 4,300 years, among the Yamnayas, a steppe people who ravaged Denmark[2] about 5,000 years ago. This discovery was made by a team of 21 researchers and published in Science (Science Advances, March 3, 2023).
So we can say that before 2,300 BCE, the people of the seven rivers moved on foot, by boat, by cart or by chariot, but not on horseback.

Another clue, and not the least: spoked wheels. The oldest trace comes from Merhgarh (Pakistan) and dates from 4,500 to 3,600 BCE[3]. It is an amulet representing a spoked wheel. Now Merhgarh is located on the territory of the Civilization of the 7 Rivers.

Here are some examples of shlokas that talk about it:

---

[1] The "colony" of Shortugai, in northern Afghanistan, was isolated from the rest of civilization and supplied it with copper and tin.
[2] And not the whole of Europe, contrary to what was announced in 2021.
[3] https://medium.com/@snehal_45125/why-we-cant-say-who-invented-the-wheel-1d594c7e58e

*1.134.11 – Formed of twelve spokes[1], not hidden, the original wheel[2] circles the Sky, following the Order. Here stood, in pairs, seven hundred and twenty cords.*

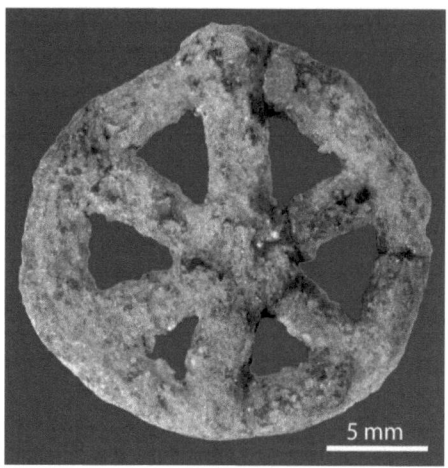

Amulet representing a spoked wheel, found in Merhgarh

*1.88.2 – With their bay or rather tawny Horses that advance their chariots, they go in Splendor, shining like gold and equipped with Lightning. O Earth, has the rim[3] of the Chariot plowed you?*

*1.164.48 – Twelve spokes feed a wheel[4], three are the eyes, who has understood it? There are three hundred and sixty spokes[5] united, which cannot be prevented from turning.*

Incidentally, we can note that there is no shortage of allusions to astronomy.

Other interesting information: weapons:

Metal weapons are not yet fully widespread.

---

[1] Twelve months.
[2] The year.
[3] Who says rim, says spoked wheel.
[4] The year, the wheel of the seasons.
[5] The days.

*10.60.4 – He dominates the peoples, like buffaloes, those who have metal weapons and those who do not, in battles.*

Arrows with metal tips were not yet widespread. Metal was expensive at this time.

*5.54. 3 – The Maruts, men impetuous as the wind, have shaken the mountains with that which shines of Light and with arrows of stone. Desiring water, in an instant they are covered with hail from a roaring, violent and very powerful assault.*

Even knife blades are not all made of metal:

*10.101.10 – Pour the flowing brownish into the wooden cups. Cut them with a large stone blade. Encircle them with ten strips. Harness the Draft Horse to the two masts.*

On the other hand, the Maruts, young gods, companions of Indra, who love to wear gold jewelry, have shiny spears.

*1.87. 3 – The Earth trembles like one who staggers when he hurries while walking on the path. When they unite in Beauty[1]. They play, roar loudly, armed with glittering spears. The Shakers[2] admire the power of the Atman[3].*

*1.167.3 – Near them there was fixed, well placed, a spear, shining like clarified butter, having the appearance of gold. The Word is like a woman honored in public, when men go into an assembly as into a cave.*

Now, nowhere in the Rig Veda is there any mention of a mixture of metals. If this mixture (bronze) had been known, we would have found it repeatedly in the metaphors of the hymns to Agni or Soma.

I gather that these glittering spears were made of copper. Ceremonial spears that are quite consistent with the Maruts wearing gold chains and other jewelry.

---

[1] In Brahman.
[2] The Maruts.
[3] The individual soul. The Self.

However, arrows with metal tips already exist:

*4.27.3 – When did the eagle roar from Heaven, or when did it carry away the generous one, when did he who bends his bow, by his spirit, send him his brilliant and terrifying arrow?*

*1.121.9 – You have shot the metal arrow brought by the sages with your leather sling[1], then, you who are invoked by many, you have struck Shushna, for the sake of Kutsa with innumerable destructive arrows .*

And they also used poisoned arrows[2]:

*6.75.15 – This one[3] is coated with poison, having a deer horn[4], whose mouth is made of metal. Here is a broad homage to the divine arrow born of the rain.*

So, these are some elements that indicate to us that these events took place before the Bronze Age which appears in North-West India shortly after the appearance of the first cities, therefore, around 3500 BCE.

Roughly speaking, we can say that the early part[5] of the Rig Veda, or the composition of the hymns of this period, takes place between 4000 BCE[6] and 3500 BCE.

Indeed, some hymns were composed well after these events took place, including contemporary elements. These hymns tell stories that happened in the past, and were passed down from generation to generation. It is therefore not at all im possible that events dating back several centuries were the subject of hymns later. Our current religions are based on books telling stories that are several thousand years old. (Bible, Koran, Torah, Mâhâbhârata, etc.).
So the ideal would be to find a specific date that could help us. Like an eclipse, for example.

---

[1] But why shoot arrows with a slingshot?
[2] Probably for hunting.
[3] The arrow.
[4] A tip.
[5] That is, mandalas 2 to 7.
[6] Or even more.

That's good! There are several allusions to an eclipse in the Rig Veda, including one that is the subject of a very important myth: the theft of cows by the Panis.

Were there several or were they talking about the same one? It's impossible to know.

*10.27. 20 – These two oxen of death, have been yoked for me, do not drive them away. Let them stop now. The waters have reached the goal of this one and the eclipse has hidden the sun which reappears.*

And above all, we have the 5.40 which is very explicit:

*5.40.5 – When, O Sun, Svarbhânu[1] Âsura[2] pierced you with darkness, the living beings remained perplexed, not knowing ignorance.*

*5.40.6 – When, O Indra, you understood the magic of Svarbhânu who fell from Heaven, Atri with her four hymns discovered the sun, hidden by darkness, by the impious.*

*5.40.8 – The mantra having united the stones, worshipping the gods by homage, and fulfilling it[3]. Atri placed the eye of Surya[4] in the Sky and hid the magics of Svarbhanu.*

*5.40.9 – This is the sun with which Svarbhânu Âsura pierced the darkness, the one that the Atris[5] found, no one else could do it.*

But, let us return to the myth of the theft of cows by the Panis. Pani means miser, greedy, money-grubber, etc. Cows symbolize Light, according to Sri Aurobindo[6]. Indeed, at that time money did not exist. People paid in cows. For example, the soma, necessary for sacrifices, cost a cow. The priests were paid in cows. The bank accounts of the time were herds of cows. The cow therefore symbolized wealth.

---

[1] Lit.: "bright sky or rays of the sun."
[2] Lit.: "divine, spiritual."
[3] Performing the sacrifice.
[4] The sun.
[5] The spiritual or non-spiritual children of Atri.
[6] The Secret of the Veda, Sri Aurobindo. Fayard 1975.

Now for an Indian, what is valid for the Earth is valid for Heaven, and vice versa. So, material wealth also means, in metaphors, spiritual wealth. And the greatest spiritual wealth that we can know is Light, Enlightenment.

The Panis, after stealing the cows, hid them in a cave in the mountain. The god Brihaspati[1], passing by, hears the cows mooing through the rocks, he breaks the cave, frees the cows and the Light returns.

*10.68.4 – Sprinkling honey on the matrix of truth, throwing forth a ray of Light like a meteorite falling from the Sky, Brihaspati, when he brought out the Cows from the stone, split the skin of the Earth, like a wave.*

*10.68.5 – By his Light he drove away the darkness of the intermediate world, as the wind drives away water. Brihaspati touched the skin of the cave, as the wind touches the clouds, and brought out the Cows.*

*10.68.6 – When Brihaspati destroyed the weak hiding place of Vala[2], who was mocking him, he took them by his hymns burning like fire, as the tongue takes food trapped by the teeth. He ate them[3] like food served and made the Cows visible.*

*10.68.9 – This one has found the Dawn, the Sky, Agni. He has driven away darkness with Light. Brihaspati has extracted the cattle from the cave, like the marrow of the bones from the joints.*

*10.68.10 – Like the forests complaining about their leaves stolen by winter, Vala lamented for the Cows liberated by Brihaspati. He did one action, not a small one, only once: he made the Sun and the Moon rise together.*

*10.68.11 – Like a dark Horse, with pearls, the fathers placed the stars in the Sky. In the night, Brihaspati, placed the most of the Light of the day, breaking the stone, he found the Cows.*

---

[1] An other name for Indra.
[2] The cave considered a demon.
[3] He kidnapped them and released them.

*10.108.5 – (Pani) These are the Cows you were looking for. They have fallen from the limits of Heaven for a good part. Who will give them back to us without a fight? Our weapons are sharp.*

*10.168.5 – Having invincible weapons, the slayer of Vritra, by the destruction of the Dâsa, has sharpened those whom he hunts. Frightened by the thunderbolt of Indra, the splendid Dawns have come out, through the opening, abandoning their chariot .*

*1.93.4 – Agni, Soma, when you have magnificently robbed the Panis[1] of their food and their Cows, you have vanquished the children of Brisaya[2], you have found the Light, the One[3] for many.*

Usually, eclipse specialists like to give a historical reminder when they write a book[4] about them. And the oldest total eclipse in all of history that humanity can remember is the one mentioned in the oldest book in the world: the Rig Veda.

Our eclipse has therefore been dated by supercomputers: it dates from February 19, 3929 BCE.

Check out this link and you'll see that this magnificent eclipse couldn't be more beautiful. It travels up the Indus, and peaks in Ladakh:

https://ssp.imcce.fr/forms/solar-eclipses/-3929

So on February 19, 3929 BCE in Harappa, it was pitch black.

Another method of calculation, the Indian method, gives 3928. The difference is explained by the Christian calendars, which the Indians do not take into account since they have their own.
Christian calendars were adjusted in the time of Julius Caesar, following an over sight of a few hours in the calculation of the length of a year.

---

[1] Demons: lit.: "greedy".
[2] A demon.
[3] Brahman, All, Moksha, immortality, non-duality…
[4] Eclipses Totales, Pierre Guillermier and Serge Koutchmy ed. Masson. 1998.

So here we are, fixed on the beginning of this civilization. We will see later that other, older events probably also occurred, but with less precision.
This civilization therefore began, before the construction of cities, around 4,000 BCE, or even much earlier.

## When did it end?

There, it will be more difficult, because the Rig Veda ends before the end of civilization. Which is quite normal.

To clarify this point, we are obliged to study geography. Not to know where it took place, we already know that: between the Ganges and the Indus.

The ruins of the big cities, like Monhenjo-Daro, Rakhi Garhi, Harappa etc. tell us that they were evacuated around 1,900 BCE[1]. But, their writing, not deciphered, can tell us nothing, and in any case, the inscriptions found on seals and other artifacts are too short to tell us that.

So, let's look at the rivers: We saw that they are mentioned in 10.75:

*10.75.5 – Join in my praise, O Ganges, O Yamuna, O Sarasvatî[2], O Shutudrî[3], O Parushnî[4]. With the Asiknî[5], with the Marudvridha[6], with the Vitastata[7], listen with those who love the Soma in the cup.*

---

[1] In Gujarat it lasted five centuries longer.
[2] Today: Ghaggar in India and Hakra in Pakistan.
[3] Today the Sutlej.
[4] Today: the Râvî.
[5] Lit.: "the black one". A river, a tributary of the Indus.
[6] Lit.: "who rejoices in the wind."
[7] Tributary of the Indus, today the Jhelum.

## The 7 Rivers Civilization

*0.75.6 – You are the first who comes together with the Susartu, the Rasâ, the Shvestya[1]. You come, O Indus, on the good chariot with those who come: the Kubha[2], the Gomatî[3], the Krumu[4], the Mehatnû[5].*

5 speaks of large rivers, while 6 speaks only of smaller ones which were small tributaries of the Indus.

And right away, we see that one is missing: the Drishadvatî, the tributary of the Sarasvatî which received the Yamuna. This one was diverted from its course by an earthquake. We do not know exactly when. On the other hand, we know where: a place in the Himalayas called: "the tear of the Yamuna".

The Drishadvati is mentioned in another older mandala:

*3.23.4 – He has installed you in the enclosure of the Earth, in the seat of Ilâ, in the Light of days. O Agni, shine richly in Men, in the Drishadvatî[6] and in the waves of the Sarasvatî[7].*

This river is therefore dried up, and its bed is still visible today. Like the Sarasvatî, it flows a little during the monsoon. It is now called the Chautang.

But, of course, we have much more interesting: The Sarasvatî- today the Ghaggar - on which the largest cities of this eastern part of this civilization were, and still are installed, Rakhi Garhi, Banawali, Kalibangan , Ganweriwala etc.

Today, it too has dried up. Like the Drishadvati, it flows a little in summer during the monsoon, but it has nothing to do with the majestic river that was the only one of all rivers to be a goddess.

---

[1] Tributary rivers of the Indus.
[2] The Kabul River. Tributary of the Indus.
[3] Lit.: "who has cows". Tributary of the Indus.
[4] Tributary of the Indus.
[5] Tributary of the Indus.
[6] "full of rocks"
[7] These are the two rivers that border the Brahmavarta (country of Brahman) where the Vedic civilization was born.

*6.52. 6 – Indra is the nearest, he comes with pleasure, thanks to his help. Sarasvatî swells with the rivers. Parjanya[1] delights us as well as the plants. Agni, who is good to call, is pleasant to invoke like a father.*

*7.96.1 – I sing the divine word: it is the broadest of rivers. Glorify Sarasvatî, O Vasistha, with good hymns and, with praises, Heaven and Earth.*

*7.95.1 – She springs forth, surging, refreshing, that Sarasvatî who wears a purifying metallic armor. She goes, like a hasty chariot, surpassing all the waters of other rivers.*

*1.164. 49 – Thy bosom, the source of pleasure, ever abundant with which thou makest prosper that which is precious, giver of Wealth, bestower of Treasure, generous, bestowing munificence, is here, Sarasvatî, the primordial element.*

These few examples must be completed by the excellent book by Michel Danino: *The lost river. On the trail of the Sarasvatî. Penguin books.* He has dissected all the scientific studies, in several fields, and brought them together in this fascinating book.

There is one thing that ethnocentric Westerners forget: they are not the only ones on Earth who are great scientists. India trains 350,000 engineers per year[2], according to some studies, and 1.5 million according to others[3]. These are people trained in the best schools. Many of them are interested in their history and their past. Many studies are conducted in geology, hydrology, seismology and other disciplines…

There is no shortage of studies on the Sarasvatî. And everyone agrees that it dried up around 1,900 BCE[4].

Here are some opinions from different disciplines:

---

[1] The deified cloud.
[2] According to the National Research Agency
[3] Julien Einaudi, Ortec
[4] https://www.hindustantimes.com/india-news/researchers-say-drying-of-saraswati-like-river-led-to-decay-of-harappan-city/story-OVBTbN5e8iEOj0aU8s11WK.html

*Michel Danino (Historian and archaeologist)*
"The drying up of the Sarasvatî River, which is believed to have occurred around 1900 BCE, marks a significant transformation of the landscape of northwest India, influencing the migration patterns of the Harappan civilization."
Danino, Michel. *The Lost River: On the Trail of the Sarasvatî* . Penguin Books India, 2010.

R. Rajaram *(Geologist) "Geological evidence suggests that the Sarasvatî River, a major river in the northwestern part of the Indian subcontinent, began to dry up around 1900 BCE, probably due to tectonic shifts and changes in monsoon patterns."*
Rajaram, R. *"Geological History of the Sarasvatî River." Journal of South Asian Geology* , vol. 15, no. 2, 2005, pp. 123-135.

*David Frawley (Indologist) "Around 1900 BCE, the Sarasvatî River, once a major river system in Vedic times, began to dry up, profoundly affecting the civilizations that thrived along its banks."*
*Frawley, David. The Rig Veda and the History of India . Aditya Prakashan, 2001.*

So, we can say that the 7 Rivers Civilization started around 4,000 BCE (or even later) and ended around 1,900 BCE following the drying up of the Sarasvatî. It will continue, as we have seen above, for another 4 or 5 centuries in Gujarat.

# The great myths

Usually when we are interested in an ancient civilization, we seek to decipher the great myths, which are based, each time, on very ancient events. The myth is very practical for oral transmission.

The Rig Veda contains several. Here are the most important ones, which we will find in several mandalas, including the oldest ones: the murder of Vritra by Indra; the war against Shambara and the Dasyus; the war against Shushna and the theft of cows by the Panis.

We have already seen that the latter tells us about an eclipse dated 3,929[1] BCE. So let's look at the others and start with the murder of Vritra.

\*\*\*

## Vritra

The root of this name means: to hide, to cover. Vritra is also often called a serpent.

*1.32. 5 – Indra struck Vritra, the darkest, with his mighty and deadly Thunderbolt. He tore him to pieces, like a tree trunk with the axe, and the serpent lies stretched out on the Earth.*

*1.32.11 – The wives of Dâsa[2], having the serpent as their guardian, were besieged, like the Cows by the Panis[3]. The Waters had been placed in a cavern, the slayer of Vritra freed them.*

Vritra holds back the waters, prevents the rivers from flowing:

---
[1] Or 3928 according to the Indian method.
[2] Impious, brigand.
[3] Lit., "misers."

*1.32. 6 – Like one who has no enemy, the arrogant one has challenged the great hero, the exterminator who torments many. He could not avoid the impact of the blows, the enemy of Indra has damaged the Rivers.*

*1.32.12 – You were like the tail of the Horse, O God Indra, you struck that individual with your thunderbolt. You gained the Light, you gained the Soma, O Hero, you freed the seven Rivers that flow downwards.*

*1.52.2 – Like a mountain firm on its base, immovable, having a thousand protectors, he has increased his Forces. When Indra slew Vritra[1] who oppressed the ascending Rivers, he made the Waves stand up against the Darkness.*

*1.52.6 – The Light has shone around you. The Force is on the move. Seated at the base of the Intermediate World[2], the Waters are obstructed. Then, O Indra, you have slain Vritra, who contains Evil, with your swift and terrible weapon, the thunder.*

*1.54.10 – Darkness reigned, the Waters, were held in the belly of Vritra[3], like a mountain shaking on its base, Indra struck the Rivers and sent them all away into the mountains.*

*1.56.5 – When, with force, you firmly fixed that which was hidden in every quarter of Heaven, through the Intermediate Space, then O Indra, in the constant excitement of intoxication, you struck Vritra and released the Waters into the Ocean.*

So, at first glance, it seems that Vitra is a cloud that prevents the rain from falling. Apparently, there is nothing extraordinary about it. So why make a myth out of it?

Is this a hint of a drought? A monsoon gone haywire? Or is it something else?

---

[1] The darkness that hides the Light of day and the ignorance that prevents Enlightenment.
[2] The world between that of Brahman: Heaven, and that of daily life, Earth;
[3] Darkness. Here it is represented as a black cloud.

In 5,300 BCE, a massive underwater volcano, the largest in human history, erupted off the coast of Japan[45].

*Masayuki Nakagawa (Volcanologist) "The eruption of Kikai Caldera, one of the largest known eruptions in Japanese history, occurred about 7,300 years ago (around 5300 BCE), significantly impacting the environment and ancient populations.*
Nakagawa, Masayuki. *"Geological and Geochemical Characteristics of the Kikai Caldera Eruption." Journal of Volcanology and Geothermal Research , vol. 178, no. 3, 2008, pp. 276-292.*

*Ta tsuo Kaneko (Geologist) "The massive volcanic eruption of the Kikai caldera, dated to around 5300 BCE, had profound effects on the climate and human settlements of the region, demonstrating the far-reaching impacts of supervolcanic activity."*
Kaneko, Tatsuo. *"Impact of the Kikai Caldera Eruption on Prehistoric Human Activity." Bulletin of the Volcanological Society of Japan , vol. 53, no. 1, 2009, pp. 112-125.*

When we know the famous Icelandic volcano, Eyjafjöll which blocked all European air traffic in 2010, we can imagine that this super-volcano obstructed the In dian sky by impressing the populations. Of course, we do not have certainty, but let's keep it in mind...

Now let us look at the Myth of Shushna.

\*\*\*

# Shushna

This word means arid[3]. Indian Sanskritists say that it symbolizes dryness.

---

[4] https://www.science-et-vie.com/nature-et-environnement/d-apres-cette-etude-la-plus-grosse-eruption-volcanique-de-l-histoire-a-eu-lieu-il-y-a-7300-ans-128108.html
[5] https://www.bluewin.ch/fr/infos/faits-divers/un-supervolcano-au-japon-100-millions-de-people-threatened-63051.html
[3] The root means dry up.

*1.112. 7 – With these you have given to Suchanti[2] wealth and a happy home, and the bearable scorching heat to Atri[3]. With these you have saved Prishnigu[4] and Purukutsa [5]. Come, O Ashvins, with these aids by which one obtains Happiness.*

*1.152. 7 – O Gods, Mitra and Varuna, with our homage and pleasures, receive this offering which procures Satisfaction[6]. May our hymn make us victorious in battles, may the divine Rain help us to cross[7].*

He is presented as an enemy, at the head of an army.

*1.51. 11 – When Indra was inspired by the zealous hymns, he mounted his chariot drawn by his two Horses which went as fast as possible. The Mighty One poured water into the dry riverbed and destroyed the fortified city of Shushna.*

*2.19.6 – Suddenly, to his charioteer, he subjected Shushna, the voracious one who creates bad harvests, to Kutsa, and Indra, for Divodâsa, destroyed the ninety-nine cities of Shambara.*

*8.40.10 – Sharpen him with good living hymns, he the impetuous one, who must be celebrated with verses, and now let him break the testicles of Shushna, by his strength, and gain the celestial waters. Let them kill all the others!*

8,200 years ago (6200 BCE), a terrible drought, accompanied by a sudden cooling, struck the entire northern hemisphere. The duration of this event is estimated at between two and four centuries. It caused enormous population movements, everywhere in the northern hemisphere, going so far as to completely depopulate certain regions, and is probably the agent of the deployment of the Neolithic. Let us keep this in mind....

*"The 8200 year BP cooling period is one of the best-documented sudden climate events of the Holocene, characterized by a rapid decrease in surface tempera-*

---

[2] A man protected by the Ashvins.
[3] A rishi. Lit.: "the devourer".
[4] A man. Lit.: "spotted".
[5] A rishi descended from Angiras.
[6] The Brahman.
[7] The trials of life.

*tures in the Northern Hemisphere and significant changes in precipitation patterns."*
Alley, RB, & Ágústsdóttir, AM (2005). The 8k event: cause and consequences of a major Holocene abrupt climate change. Quaternary Science Reviews, 24(10-11), 1123-1149.

*"Paleoclimatic records indicate that the 8200 year BP event was marked by a major drought phase in many regions of the world, affecting emerging civilizations and altering natural landscapes."*
Rohling, E.J., & Pälike, H. (2005). Centennial-scale climate cooling with a sudden cold event around 8,200 years ago. Nature, 434(7036), 975-979.

*"Climate changes occurring 8,200 years ago, characterized by marked cooling and reduced precipitation, have been identified from multiple paleoclimate archives, including ice cores, lake sediments, and tree rings."*
Thomas, EK, et al. (2007). Centennial-scale climate variability during the Holocene in northwestern North America. Geology, 35(8), 681-684.

Nevertheless, descriptions of droughts are numerous, because another one would strike much later, around 2200 BCE, that is to say in the middle of the mature phase of civilization. We will come back to this.

*4.25. 7 – Indra is not friendly with the rich, nor with the miserly, nor with those who do not prepare soma. He loves the drinkers of soma. He presses for knowledge, and destroys dryness. He manifests exclusively to the soma preparer.*

*4.28. 5 – It is very true, you two, Indra and Soma, you have watered the vast pasture of the Horses and the Cows. You have pierced the rock that dried up the fields and you have emptied it.*

*4.22. 7 – Here, of course, Master of the reddish ones, with your helps, the sisters, the goddesses sacrifice, when he has released the waters that had been driven away long ago, to flow along their course.*

\*\*\*

# Shambara

With Shambara we enter into a controversy. It is this myth that gave Max Müller the idea that the Indians could not have written all their books, since the only ones who were civilized were the Westerners. He therefore thought that, since Sanskrit and the European languages were of the same nature, it was necessarily because the Westerners had come to bring, by their strength and superior intelligence, Sanskrit, the Indian gods, and all of Indian culture.

And all this, of course, justified the colonization of India by the British. It was necessary to put back on the right path these almost ancestors, who had mixed with the impure indigenous races.

Shambara was the chief of the Dasyus, the enemies of Divodâsa[1], the king of the Bharatas, grandfather of Sudâsa who would later distinguish himself in the war of the ten kings.

Shambara rules over a hundred fortified "cities[2]". Indra helps Divodâsa to fight him and destroy these cities.

*1.130.7 – For the Pûrus, you destroyed with your thunderbolt ninety strongholds[3], for Divodâsa[4], your great servant, O Dancer, your servant, with your thunderbolt. For Atithigva[5], the Strong One brought Shambara[6] down from the mountain, distributing the great Riches with his Strength, all the great Riches with his Strength.*

---

[1] "servant of Heaven".
[2] The Sanskrit word is Pura, which today means city (Jaïpur, Udaïpur) but which can also mean: stronghold, fortress, fortified camp....
[3] Anything that prevents Enlightenment.
[4] Lit.: "servant of Heaven".
[5] Lit.: "invited by the Cows".
[6] A demon.

*2.14.6 – Priests, to him who, as with a stone, destroyed the hundred cities of Shambara, who brought to Earth the hundred thousand sons of Varcin[1], bring this soma to Indra.*

*2.19.3 – (Indra speaks) In my intoxication I destroyed the ninety-nine cities of Shambara and the hundredth, his house, all together, when I helped Divodâsa Atithigva[2].*

As we have seen above, Shambara is the chief of the Dasyus (or Dâsas).

## The Dasyus (or Dâsas)

Etymology tells us that this word comes from the root *das* = to exhaust, or to be in lack of...
These are the bad guys, those who have no god. They have all the faults, and of course in spiritual metaphors, they represent everything that prevents enlightenment (hatred, hypocrisy, jealousy etc.). Basically, for an Ârya, they are less than nothing.

*10.22.8 – The Dasyu is a lazy, an ignorant, a non-human, whose rules are different. You the slayer of enemies, destroy the weapon of the Dâsa.*

*1.51. 8 – Know the difference between the Âryas and the Dasyus, punish those who are lawless, send those who want to command us to the destruction of the powerful one who sacrifices on the sacrificial grass. Be satisfied quickly with intoxication.*

*1.59. 6 – I must now invoke the power of that vigorous god whom the children of Pûru[3] associate with the slayer of Vritra[4]. Agni, Vaishvânara, has driven away the Dasyus[5], the abject, the impious, far away in different directions and dismembered Shambara.*

---

[1] A demon.
[2] Lit.: "to whom one must go".
[3] Name of the Vedic confederation. They lived on both banks of the Sarasvatî.
[4] Darkness. Vritra's Killer: Indra.
[5] Brigands, impious.

And then, these Dasyus have the supreme defect for our racist Westerners[1]: they have black skin.

*1.130.8 – Indra, in battles, protects the Noble one who makes sacrifices, he who has a hundred helps, in all fights, in all fights, he wins the Light of Heaven. By vanquishing the impious with black skin, punishing the enemies of Manu. Skillful, he burns all the greedy, he burns the malevolent.*

*9.41.1 – Those who support us, have come, like Cows, agile, vehement, they have advanced, killing those who have black skin.*

This is not all, these Dasyus, or Dâsas, have no nose or no mouth[2].

*5.29. 10 – You have enlarged one wheel of the Sun for Kutsa, on the other, you have made space for the one who overcomes difficulties. You have killed the noseless Dasyus, by violence, in the house, those who have a hurtful word.*

The fight must have gone easily for the Âryas because the Dasyus had neither horses nor chariots.

*5.31.5 – When, for thee the Bull, the mighty and the pressing stones honour thee in harmony with Aditi, the rims have led Indra to crush the Dasyus who have no Horses and who have no chariots.*

And then, anyway, these Dasyus are inferior[3].

*1.101. 5 – He who is the Lord of that which moves and breathes, who in the Brahman first found the Cows, Indra who drove out the inferior Dasyus[4], it is from him that we ask friendship.*

---

[1] In the 19th century, all scientists who claimed to follow Darwin were sincerely racist. Not necessarily hateful, but convinced that all those who were not white were inferior.
[2] The Sanskrit word *anasa* can be translated in two ways.
[3] This is the only time this notion appears in the Rig Veda.
[4] The Dasyus, being the forces of Darkness, are necessarily inferior to the Âryas, who are the forces of Light. It is the interpretation of this concept in the first degree that gave rise to Nazism.

This myth is based, like the others, on ancient facts. Can we compare them to the natural disasters that we have just seen a little earlier?

Are these peoples from southern India, who would be in the north at that time? This thesis is supported by Dravidian activists[1].

If we accept this word "Krishna" which means black for the Dasyus, then we must also admit that among the Âryas, there was a black-skinned rishi too: Krishna Angirasa, the author of hymn 8.85 and 10.31. We also find a certain Krishna in 1.116.23, in 1.117.7. He is not a Dasyu, but an Ârya.

According to B. B. Lal, the former director of the Archaeological Survey of India, the terms "Dasyus" and "Dasas" were used as common appellations for all the enemies of the Aryas. These were not specific tribes but rather a generic term applied to any group opposed to the Aryas.

This idea seems to be the most probable, because the term Dâsa is applied to the enemies of Indra in the myths of Shambara, Shushna and Vritra, which seem to be of different periods.

---

[1] Those who speak a Dravidian language.

The 7 Rivers Civilization

## The War of the Ten Kings

We have just seen the first myths that we find in all the mandalas. We see clearly that they tell us about very ancient facts. References to individuals of whom we know nothing. Who is attacking whom? It is difficult to say. Nothing clearly indi cates any displacement of population. Which does not mean that there was none. But from there to deduce the fable of the Aryan invasion, there is a gap.

Now, let's go into History with the War of the Ten Kings. It is the first war that hu manity has a good memory of. Indeed, we know the protagonists, the places of the battles and the names of the main dead.

*7.19.9 – They came to the Parushnî, with an intention, an evil intention, surely not approaching quickly. Indra subdued the enemies, who, though in society, spoke badly and ran fast before Sudâsa.*

It was probably not a war in the style of modern wars with millions of fighters and hundreds of thousands of dead, "progress" had not yet struck. But nevertheless, there were two battles: one on the banks of the Parushni and the other on the Yamuna.

*7.19.14 – The hundred and sixty thousand[1] Anus and Druhyus, wanting Cows, fell asleep. Sixty heroes, led by six of them, honoured all the actions performed by Indra.*

*7.19.19 – The Yamuna stirred up Indra and the Tritsus. He defeated Bheda there completely, and the Âjas, the Shigrus, the Yaksus, offered tribute by striking the heads of Horses.*

The reason would be the following, according to more recent writings. King Sudâsa, grandson of Divodâsa, had as Purohita, as chaplain, Vishvamitra[2] whom he replaced by another: Vasishta[3]. Vishvamitra would not have appreciated being

---
[1] This figure is probably not to be taken literally.
[2] "friend of all".
[3] "the richer, the better."

replaced and would have united the five Vedic peoples, associated with five non-Vedic peoples and would have fought the Bharatas, although they came from the federation of Pûrus. Here are the names of these five peoples: Pûru, Yadu, Turvashas, Anu, and Druhyu.

King Sudasa won the war and then united the five peoples to found the Arya people. They would be joined by others and eventually spread across the entire Indian subcontinent.

*7.19.7 – The Pakthas[1] and the Bhalânas cried out to the Alinas, the Vishanas, the Shivas: "The feast-companions of the Âryas, who have Cows, have brought us here for the Tritsus[2], to unite men[3]."*

*7.33. 3 – Now surely it is with them that they have crossed the Indus. Now surely it is with them that he has killed Bedha[4]. Now surely it is by your mantras that Indra has favoured Sudâsa against the ten kings, O Vasishtas.*

*7.83.6 – These two call you in battles, Indra and Varuna, to bring Riches. There you protected Sudâsa, allied to the Tritsus, when he was in difficulty against the ten kings.*

*7.83.8 – Indra and Varuna, you helped Sudasa who was surrounded on all sides by the ten kings who wanted to be powerful. There, those who wear white attire, their hair braided and in a bun, by their insightful mind, the Tritsus, wanted to serve.*

This fratricidal war left its mark on people's minds and was probably the origin of the peace that would reign later; after it, there would be no more new battles. Those that we find in the more recent mandalas will always be associated with the ancient myths.

---

[1] This people would be the ancestor of the Pashtun people. According to Ka Ka Khel; Sayed Wiqar Ali Shah (2014). "Origin of the Afghans: Myths and Reality". *Journal of Asian Civilizations* . **37** (1): 189–199.
[2] "To counter the Tritsus" a branch of the Bharatas.
[3] To unite with non-Âryas.
[4] Lit.: "the one who tears".

The question arises: is it realistic for a king, conqueror of ten others, to succeed in uniting them[1] in a single society other than by force and violence?

I think I have found an answer. Not in the Rig Veda, but in the manava-dharma-sastra[2], better known in the West as the laws of Manu. Of course, this collection of laws is more recent, about 1,000 BCE, but it reflects well the spirit of the Nobles (Âryas).

*7.201 After conquering a country, let the king honour the gods worshipped there and the virtuous Brahmins; let him distribute largesse to the people and make proclamations that will remove all fear.*

Humiliating a defeated person is always a bad idea.

---

[1] To unite the Âryas only, not the non-Âryas.
[2] Translation by A. Loiseleur-Deslongchamps. Forgettenbooks.com

# Other wars between Âryas

This war of the ten kings, between Âryas and Âryas associated with non-Âryas, was not the only one during the centuries preceding the construction of the cities.

There must have been troubled periods, perhaps due to the arrival of various populations. In any case, the general impression I got[1] throughout the translation was that the Âryas were not the ones attacking, but the ones defending themselves, except perhaps in the Myth of Shambara. But I could be wrong.

These troubled periods may also be due to extreme climatic events such as droughts or natural disasters such as the Japanese volcano and the great drought of 6,200 BCE.

Here are some shlokas that talk about these preserves:

The first is taken from the oldest mandala.

*6.44.17 – Intoxicated by that one[2], kill the enemies, O Hero, whether they are relatives or strangers, the unfriendlies. Those who have weapons aimed at us, from across the bank, aiming with projectiles, O Indra. Kill them and destroy them!*

Here are two more, taken from the last mandala:

*10.38.3 – Whether it is the Dasa or the Ârya who wants to fight us, O Indra, you who are much worshipped, let these enemies be easy to fight. With you, may we conquer them in combat.*

*10.69.12 – This is the fire of Vadhryashva[3], the slayer of Vritra, ever kindled, with homage, for him who is to be honored. Stand against those who defy us, whether we are of the same family or not, O Vadhryashva[4].*

---
[1] But, I could be wrong.
[2] The soma.
[3] Another name for Indra.
[4] Who has castrated horses.

I haven't found much clear evidence of these wars, other than the Ten Kings War, which makes me think that these problems are old and must not have been frequent.

# Spirituality

As everyone knows, the Rig Veda is the basis of all Indian spirituality, whether for Hinduism, Buddhism or Jainism. And this reason appears through the metaphors, often warlike, that should be deciphered.

## The sacrifice

It was the Westerners of the 19th century who chose this name because during this "ceremony", an animal was killed and then eaten.

In Sanskrit, it is called Yajña, from the root *Yaj* which means to honor, to venerate one or more gods. An animal is indeed killed during this sacrifice, but the Rig Veda hardly mentions it. This practice, which comes directly from shamanism, will be abandoned a little later.

It should be noted, however, that Vedic sacrifices continue in some parts of India today. The killing of an animal is still practiced, causing problems of conscience among the non-violent Hindu population.

The whole life of society revolved around sacrifices. It was their great preoccupation. Sacrifices could be public or private. They could be conducted by up to sixteen priests. The richer the householder, the more priests his sacrifice had to have. The result was the same whether one was rich or poor. The goal was Enlightenment. The hiring of priests was not obligatory, and the poor could, if he wished, make a sacrifice at home, without calling on anyone.

The great public sacrifices, organized by important figures, could attract crowds, especially during the Trikadrukas. When we see, today, the Khumba Mela and the millions of people who attend it, we can get an idea of what these great sacrifices could have been.

*2.11. 17 – During the mighty and joyous Trikadrukas[1], O Mighty One, drink soma, O Indra. It flows into your beard. Come and drink the juice of soma, intoxicating for your Bay Horses.*

*2.22. 1 – During the Trikadrukas, the Great One, who has a grain-shaped head, the one who howls a lot, drank the juice of soma with Vishnu, at will. The Great One got intoxicated to do his great and wide action. Thus let the god unite with the god, the true Indra, the true Indu.*

French speakers are fortunate to have a wonderful work by Willem Caland: the Agnistoma[2] (in two volumes). Published in 1907, and available from forgottentbooks.com, it describes in detail from old treatises such as the rituals of cantors, the rituals of the Adhvaryus[3] and other texts, the entire ceremony of the Agnistoma – the praise of fire – which was the typical sacrifice, from which others, shorter or longer, developed, such as the Jyotishtoma[4], for example. It occurred, at least, once a year, on one of the full moons of spring. But, it could take place more often.

*1.94. 4 – We bring fuel and prepare offerings, gathered for you every lunar fortnight. Regulate our minds to prolong our life! O Agni, do not make us suffer in your friendship.*

The classic sacrifice of the Masters of the House was offered by the sacrificing couple. It lasted five days. The first four were intended to prepare the spirit of the sacrificers. This preparation was essential for the experience to be positive.

On the first day, the man and his wife were washed, purified, then the man was shaved of all his body hair[5] and hair. The woman was not, but she was washed by a priest. The land, on which the sacrificial area would be established, was negoti ated by the priests. They built huts, one for the man, one for the woman, another for the priests, plus a hut for the cart that had been used to bring the soma.

---

[1] The first three days of a great public sacrifice.
[2] "praise of Agni, praise of fire, praise of Light, of Enlightenment."
[3] Priests.
[4] In Praise of Light.
[5] Except pubic hair.

Then, quantities of rites and mantras rocked the finalization of the sacrificial area. All the mantras used appear in the book about Agnistoma, in the form of scores, without the musical notes[1].

The sacrificer and his wife ate only yogurt during these four days. They were not allowed to scratch themselves, if they wanted to do so, they had to use an antelope horn.

On the second day, they bought the soma plants. These were bought dried. The soma was exchanged for a cow. The next day, the plants were sorted and measured, the day after. The soma plants were lined up on a black antelope skin. For eighteen people, in the case of a large sacrifice – 16 priests plus the sacrificers – the dose was as follows: one span, plus one span minus one finger, plus one span minus two fingers, plus one span minus three fingers. In total, the line of soma plants retained was about one cubit long. On the fourth day, the soma was left to "swell" in a container full of water all night.

The night before the soma was consumed, the sacrificers and priests did not sleep. They spent the night playing dice to avoid falling asleep.

On the fifth day, at dawn, the sacrifice began again. The priests lit the fires. Then they took half of the plants for the morning pressing. The rest was divided in two, for the midday and evening pressings.

Before the sun began to rise, they pressed the soma, and drank it, facing the East. Of course, everything took place with mantras taken from the Rig Veda. They were sung, murmured, chanted according to very precise rules. Among these priests, the Brahman[2], supervised the whole and corrected the errors made by his colleagues.

Mantras and rites followed one another until noon. When the sun was at its zenith, they drank the juice from the second pressing and started again at sunset. The experience lasted 18 hours. Which is very long, but necessary for everything to be successful.

---

[1] Alas.
[2] This word, which is used by many, is used to designate a priest.

# The soma

The first European Indianists tore their hair out trying to understand what soma was. Some saw alcohol in it. But most saw branches, bundles of wood, since soma was brought in a cart pulled by a cow. Several plants have been announced but most modern Indianists see ephedra, a plant containing an amphetamine. The Indian variety is one of the most powerful in the world.

The Rig Veda gives only a brief description of soma: amshu. That is, fiber, filament. And it never speaks of flowers, leaves, seeds or fruit. Not once in the entire Rig Veda is it mentioned.

*Ephedra gerardiana*

But ephedra has flowers, and its stems are neither fibers nor filaments. On the other hand, the effect of ephedra, which is part of the composition of MDMA - ecstasy - has nothing to do with that of soma. Its molecule is from the amphetamine family and not the tryptamine family. It cannot help to provoke non-duality.

And then, taking amphetamines 3 times a day is very bad for your health. They can really cause a stroke or cardiac arrest.

On the other hand, psilocybes, like all mushrooms are composed of soluble fibers. And they contain up to 90% water. When dried are very long and very thin. Albert Hofmann, the discoverer of LSD, consumed them as part of his research and says in his biography[1] that in the five grams, which constitute a dose, he had 42 dried mushrooms. So, they are very thin and fine and can correspond to amshu. And of course, the molecule is a tryptamine.

*Ephedra has small flowers*

*1.142. 1 – Bring, O Agni, you who are lit, the gods today, for him who holds the ladle. Press the ancestral fiber for the pious who press the soma.*

*2.13. 1 – The season[2] is the mother of this soma plant, which, when it was born, entered quickly into the Waters[3], making it grow. It was full of flowing juice. The first juice of the fiber is accompanied by mantras.*

*5.36. 1 – Let him come here, that Indra, who knows how to give wealth and goods. Like a thirsty buffalo roaming the desert, let him drink the extract of the fiber until he satisfies his desire.*

*3.19. 2 – I bring you the luminous offering that has the power to give Light with clarity. Turning to the right, choosing the assistance of the gods, may he come to the sacrifice with his Gifts and Riches that expand him[4] totally.*

---

[1] LSD mon enfant terrible. L'esprit frappeur, Paris. 2003.
[2] The rainy season, the monsoon.
[3] Symbol of purification and streams of Light.
[4] Which broaden the mind.

Ephedra, mixed with cannabis, added with opium, was used in Turkmenistan in the Oasis Civilization, in the Karakum Desert[1]. The effect is very impressive, and one can easily create a religion with this mixture. But, in this case, we remain in duality, whereas with soma, this is not the case. It is non-duality.

Here are some shlokas that describe the effects of soma.

*2.41.4 – Mitra and Varuna, this soma juice enables one to attain the Truth. Listen here to my invocation.*

*10.9.9 – O Waters, today I have come to unite with you through juice. O Agni, come here, full of juice and flow to unite us with the Light.*

*9.113.11 – Where there is bliss, plenitude, jubilation, happiness, he sits. There, where one attains the delights of desire, make me immortal. Flow, around, for Indra, O Indu.*

*1.4.2 – Come to our soma pressing, you soma drinker, drink! Rich intoxication truly gives Light.*

*5.81.2 – He who stands in the worlds, the immortal soma flows around them. Realizing Union and Liberation, to help us, the drops come after the Dawn like the*

---
[1] Discovery made by Viktor Sarianidi .

*sun.*

*1.15. 5 – Indra, drink soma at the auspicious time to attain Brahman[1]. Yes, your friendship is invincible.*

*6.3. 3 – The soma juice with its spotless appearance is not terrifying when it brings luminous meditation, like the powerful drops[2]. Where does this one spend a charming night in a wooden house[3]?*

*8.48. 3 – We have drunk the soma. We have become immortal. We have entered the Light, we have found the gods. What can the envious do to us now? What can the hatred of the mortal do to us, O Immortal?*

*1.191. 12 – Promoter of inner wealth, healer of sorrow, generous, developer of happiness. O Soma, you are a good friend for our existence.*

In all likelihood, the soma would indeed be a psilocybe cubensis, a mushroom containing psilocybin. It is, to my knowledge, the only entheogenic plant that fits the description: fiber, filament, and which has neither flower, nor fruit, nor seed, nor leaf.

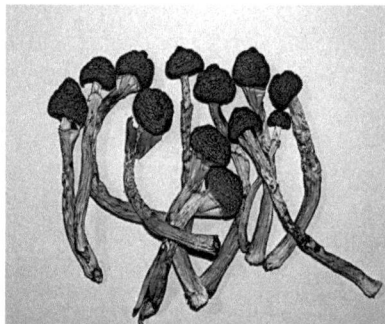

*Psilocybes cubensis*

Now psilocybin is from the same family as dimethyltryptamine, which we naturally produce in our brain, in the epiphysis – the pineal gland. This DMT[4] is acti-

---
[1] Sat-Cit-Ananda.
[2] Soma drops.
[3] Allusion to the hut built on the first day of the sacrifice for him.
[4] To simplify.

vated by various yoga techniques, including pranayama. Professor Stanislav Grof, a Czech psychiatrist, demonstrated this for decades by developing holotropic breathing[1]. This technique allows you to obtain exactly the same effect as LSD[2].

*"Holotropic breathwork can catalyze experiences that are indistinguishable from those induced by psychedelic substances, including LSD."*
*Grof, S. (1988). The Adventure of Self-Discovery: Dimensions of Consciousness and New Perspectives in Psychotherapy and Inner Exploration. SUNY Press.*

*"Over the years, we have accumulated substantial evidence showing that holotropic breathwork can reliably induce experiences that are phenomenologically identical to those elicited by psychedelic drugs."*
*Grof, S. (2000). The psychology of the future: Lessons from modern research on consciousness. SUNY Press.*

*"Holotropic breathwork can facilitate experiences that closely resemble those induced by LSD and other psychedelics. These include powerful reliving of birth, profound mystical experiences, and vivid encounters with archetypal figures."*
*Grof, S. (1993). The Holotropic Mind: The Three Levels of Human Consciousness and How They Shape Our Lives. HarperCollins.*

Having fled communism, he had taken refuge in the USA. In Czechoslovakia, he specialized in the treatment of schizophrenics. Using LSD, he made them regress to their birth and relive the traumas they had experienced at the time of childbirth. From his experiences, he developed a concept of perinatal matrices[3], as well as transpersonal psychology.

He continued his work in the USA until Richard Nixon, under pressure from fun damentalist Christian sects, launched a war against psychedelics, which were legal and the subject of medical research in the psychiatric field until then.

---

[1] LSD Psychotherapy (4th Edition): The Healing Potential of Psychedelic Medicine Paperback – April 1, 2008 by Stanislav Grof (Author), Albert Hofmann (Introduction), Andrew Weil (Foreword )
[2] The Ultimate journey Stanislav Grof 2006. Guy Tredaniel.
[3] Man's Encounter with Death " Stanislav Grof & Joan Halifax – Editions du Rocher

Continuing his treatment became impossible. So he developed his holotropic breathing. Since then, it has been practiced legally almost everywhere in Europe.

On the other hand, studies on psychedelics are multiplying in the West these days. Even in France, where drinking alcohol is considered something positive and rewarding[1], some studies, very strictly supervised, focus on Ketamine. In France, any entheogenic plant is strictly prohibited under penalty of prison, even talking about it positively can earn you a year in prison. But Ketamine does not come from an entheogenic plant, and is not from the tryptamine family[2].

In several Western countries, such as Switzerland, Portugal, the Netherlands, Canada, and parts of the United States, people suffering from problems such as depression, low self-esteem, unjustified fears, etc. are treated with psychedelics. One or two doses are enough, much to the despair of pharmaceutical companies who prefer to sell drugs to be taken every day. Business is business.
Here are some Western comments on its effects:

*"The study by Griffiths et al. (2008) showed that controlled administration of psilocybin, a psychedelic compound found in magic mushrooms, induces profound mystical experiences, characterized by a sense of oneness with the cosmos and an expansion of consciousness."*

*"Research by Carhart-Harris et al. (2016) found that psilocybin administration induced altered states of consciousness associated with perceptions of mystical unity and transcendent experiences, suggesting therapeutic potential for the treatment of psychological disorders."*

*"A recent study by Barrett et al. (2021) examined the effects of psychedelics on consciousness and found that participants reported feelings of oneness with the universe and a deep connection with nature after consuming substances like LSD and psilocybin."*

---

[1] Until 1956, red wine was served to children in school canteens in France.
[2] Elon Musk takes it every two weeks to combat his depression. It's completely ridiculous and explains a lot.

*"The work of Griffiths et al. (2016) has demonstrated that psychedelic experiences, induced by psilocybin, can lead to lasting changes in self-perception and worldview, fostering a sense of unity and interconnectedness with all that exists."*

*"A meta-analysis of several studies, conducted by Tagliazucchi et al. (2016), confirmed that controlled use of psychedelics can trigger mystical experiences and perceptions of oneness in participants, thus offering new perspectives in the understanding of consciousness and spirituality."*

Let us add that the effect produced is curiously close to what people who have had a near-death experience have felt. Here are some testimonies:

*Betty Eadie - author:*
*"During my near-death experience, I was greeted by beings of Light who showed me the beauty and love on the other side. I felt a peace and joy beyond anything I had ever known on Earth."*
Eadie, B. J. (1992). Embraced by the Light. Gold Leaf Press.

*Anita Moorjani - author and speaker:*
*"During my near-death experience, I felt enveloped in unconditional love. I realized that everything I thought was important—like career success and material possessions—was nothing compared to love. and compassion."*
Moorjani, A. (2012). Dying to Be Me: My Journey from Cancer, to Near Death, to True Healing. Hay House.

On the other hand, experiments have been carried out in the laboratory and images of the brain, under the influence of LSD [1], have been made, showing connections between different parts of the brain that are never in contact in ordinary times.

---

[1] LSD is a derivative of rye ergot whose effects became known in the Middle Ages in Europe under the name of: "Mal des Ardents" in France and Ergotism in the United Kingdom.

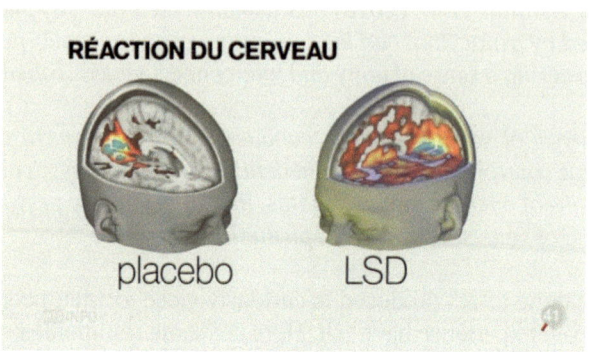

@lesoir.be

We can therefore affirm, without the slightest doubt, that drinking soma was neither insignificant nor anecdotal. Especially since the sacrificers only ate yogurt for four days and did not sleep the night before consuming the soma[1].

Drinking soma therefore had a considerable importance on the whole society. The disappearance of excess ego[2], in all the leaders of the society, also makes disappear the feeling of superiority, violence, greed, contempt and everything that sets humans against each other.

Society could therefore only be peaceful, turned towards spirituality, towards "living together", in the general interest.

Archaeology amply demonstrates this: there is not the slightest trace of violence anywhere, neither in the ruins, nor in the representations of individuals, nor on the skeletons in the cemeteries. Not the slightest monument to the glory of this one or that one, no bas-reliefs showing prisoners, nor of "valiant warriors", no display of luxury, either.

Vainglory and vanity were not on the menu of the Seven Rivers Civilization.

---

[1] Fasting and sleep deprivation alone can cause this Enlightenment in some people.
[2] Disappearance is not final for all individuals. For those with a too strong ego, such as politicians, a suitable environment is essential, or the renewal of the experience must take place at the very least every year.

## Religion or Pure Spirituality

When you talk about spirituality to an ordinary Westerner, he understands religion[1]. But, of course, there is a huge difference between these two terms. Religion is: you have to believe in one or more gods, have faith. Otherwise, things will go very badly for you. You will roast in hell for eternity or you will be reincarnated as a stray dog.

The people must observe rules dictated by the god(s). These are extremely strict rules that are, in reality, written by men, for the functioning of society.

In the Rig Veda, with the exception of the 10th mandala, which we will return to later, the equivalent of the Tablets of the Law practically does not exist. Indeed, you will not find anywhere, in the first nine mandalas, rules of morality to be followed imperatively.

Here is an exception.

*7.89. 6 – It is not one's own intelligence nor falsehood, O Varuna, but alcohol, stupidity, dice, heedlessness. The younger is a humiliation to the older. Surely sleep is not the one that expels error.*

The practice of sacrifice was sufficient for the sacrificing couple to know what they had to do without needing "divine" laws, established by humans.

## The goal to be achieved for each

The Rig Veda is the basis of almost all Indian spiritual practices: Hinduism, Buddhism, Jainism. They are all based on the same principle: human beings can become aware of the Ultimate Reality during their lifetime.

This Ultimate Reality, which we become aware of through what I call Enlightenment, for want of having found another more suitable word, is called Brahman in

---

[1] And in France, the word "spiritual" means: having a sense of humor.

India and Nirvana among the Buddhists. But outside these countries, we do not find suitable words in our Western languages.

In India, this Ultimate Reality is called: Brahman. This word comes from the root bṛh which means: to grow, to increase...

So this was the goal to be achieved by each householder. They did not have exclusivity, far from it. Everyone could access it, but householders were required to do so, since they had to make decisions that concerned the entire population. It was, of course, out of the question to give the keys to society to anyone with an inflated ego.

# The three worlds

Unlike us Westerners, the Âryas lived not in one world, like us, but in three worlds at the same time: Earth, Heaven and the Intermediate World.

Western translators have called the latter: the Atmosphere. Yes, of course it is, but it is much more.

Earth is our ordinary state of mind. The everyday one. Heaven is Enlightenment and the Intermediate World is everything in between.

This principle of division into three is found everywhere in Vedism and its descendants: Sat-Cit-Ananda, the trimurti, the trident of Shiva, the dosha kings of Ayurveda, the three gunas[1] which create matter... And even in Christianity which some claim to be an indirect descendant of Vedism[2]: the Father, the Son and the Holy Spirit....

Spiritual experiences, apart from being strictly intimate and personal, are diverse and varied. They all take place in the Intermediate World, except the Supreme Experience, which we cannot describe and still less explain, which takes place in the third world: Heaven.

---
[1] Qualities, in the primary sense of the term.
[2] Abraham resided in Ur, in Sumer, where there was a strong Vedic presence.

## How the society works

Being rich gives power. The Masters of the House were the rich of that time. They were the ones who had the power. So they had to drink the soma. It was **THE** rule, the only rule of the Âryas.

And, of course, a civilization in which all householders drink a powerful psychedelic[1] regularly cannot be an ordinary civilization.

*1.12.6 – Agni is inflamed by Agni, young poet, Master of the House, he carries the offering with the spoon of soma to the mouth.*

*1.151.2 – When these, the people of Purumîlha[2], who possess the soma, as friends have given you Knowledge, now it shines on the path and, O Mighty Ones, the householder has heard it.*

*7.1.1 – Men generated Agni, with the flames[3] of the arani, by the two active hands and recitations, making them visible from afar, enlightening the householder.*

*8.31.5 – The master couple, unanimously, squeeze and make it flow, mixed with the milk, by themselves.*

*10.61.7 – When the father jumped upon his daughter, uniting with her, he spread his flood upon the Earth. The gods generated the mantra, giving good Wealth, and sculpted the householder, protector of the law.*

---

[1] With an effect that lasts 18 hours!
[2] "abundant liquid": the soma.
[3] Or with the sparks of the arani.

## The 7 Rivers Civilization

When those in charge of society are primarily interested in their spirituality, there is no war[1], no violence, no gross inequality, no sub-humans, as was the case in other civilizations[2].

*1.100.9 – With his left hand he contains the mighty, with his right hand he holds together actions. He obtains Wealth even for the poor. May Indra and the Maruts be our protection.*

*4.25. 7 – Indra is not friendly with the rich, nor with the miserly, nor with those who do not prepare soma. He loves the drinkers of soma. He presses for knowledge, and destroys dryness. He manifests Himself exclusively to the preparer of soma.*

A spiritual civilization, in which there is no army, no slave, no centralization or authoritarianism, is a civilization focused on the happiness of its people. The leaders, having dissolved their ego, have no desire to go to war with their neighbors and generate misery and death. In the event of conflict with one people or another, or internal problems, they prefer negotiation and discussion to brutality and war.

---

[1] Which is confirmed by archaeology. No traces of war have been found anywhere, at any level.
[2] And this is, unfortunately, still the case, everywhere on Earth.

## The place of women

This civilization could not be macho. The man and the woman offer the sacrifice together. Women drink the soma like men. They are not relegated to the kitchen, or considered secondary.

*9.61.18 – O Purified One, your juice is effective. It reigns luminously. The Light is seen by one and all.*

*9.38.4 – This one[1], like an eagle, flies among humans and sits in houses, going to man and woman.*

*5.46. 8 – Let these ladies, the wives of the gods, pursue him[2], Indrânî, Agnâyî, Ashvinî. Let Heaven and Earth and Varunânî listen to us. Let the goddesses pursue, it is the time of women.*

*10.159. 2 – I am the Light, I am the leader, I am the powerful decider. My husband, whom I have conquered, must follow my intention by obeying.*

Several women rishis composed hymns: Romasâ, Lopamudrâ, Apalâ, Kadrû, Visvavarâ, Ghoshâ, Juhû, Vagambhrinî, Paulomî, Yamî, Indranî, Savitrî, and De vajamî.

So, the woman was not considered inferior and just good for making children. Which is in agreement with other small civilizations, like that of Karakum and that of the Oxus.

*5.61.6 – And a woman is more trustworthy than a man, if he does not follow the gods and is selfish.*

*10.86.10 – Until then, the woman was the companion of the invoker, or had to go away. Now she is seen as the woman of truth, to be the wise mistress of Indra, and this is rejoicing. Indra is above all.*

---

[1] The soma.
[2] Continue the sacrifice.

Even though the man is the head of the family, the woman is not mistreated, nor subjected to the puritanism of men, as is still the case today on almost the entire planet. The statuettes found in the ruins show that women, like men, go bare-chested. This demonstrates that a broad open-mindedness reigned.

*6.64. 2 – Fortunately, you have appeared. You illuminate from afar. Your flame and your lights have risen towards the Sky. You show your breasts while progressing in beauty, goddess Dawn, in great splendors.*

*10.18. 7 – These women, not widows, having a good husband, made up[1] with clarified butter, let them enter together. Without tears, without affliction, let the women rise to the Treasury, in the ancient matrix[2].*

*10.85.26 – Let Pushan lead you out of here by taking your hand. Let the Ashvins bring you in their chariot. Go home since you are the mistress of the house. It is not him, it is you who has knowledge.*

*10.85.27 – Prosper here with your dear offspring, awaken to be the mistress of the house, in this house. Free your body with your husband, since you announce the ancient knowledge.*

*10.85.45 – Make this woman, O generous Indra, have good sons, a good portion. Give her ten sons. Make her husband the eleventh.*

It was good to be a woman in the 7 Rivers Civilization.

---

[1] Eye makeup. Clarified butter is used for everything in India.
[2] The Brahman.

# Manners

Knowing the customs of a 4,000 year old civilization whose writing has not been deciphered is usually almost impossible, but thanks to metaphors, we will be able to get an idea.

## The funeral

If today the vast majority of Indians are cremated, there are certain exceptions: the non-Hindus, the very poor, who are thrown directly into the river[1] for lack of money to pay for the wood, and sâdhus and other renunciants. The latter are buried. Buried sitting for the sâdhus.

In the Rig Veda, these two formulas were also applied.

*10.16.1 – Do not burn this one, O Agni, do not afflict him, do not destroy his skin or his body. When you prepare him, O Jâtavedas, but rather send him, to the Fathers.*

*10.16.2 – When you have burnt him, then, Jâtavedas, send him to the Fathers. When he goes to another life, then he will be the one who fulfills the will of the gods.*

As you can see, the last shloka quoted here hints at another life. Probably a reincarnation. This is confirmed in these other shlokas:

*10.14. 12 – The two messengers of Yama, enjoying the lives of others, with extensive powers, run after people. May they give us life again so that we can see the sun and today, here, happiness.*

---

[1] Today, all rivers are goddesses, and so it is good for the karma of the poor, who will be reborn less poor.

*10.15. 14 – Those who have been burned by Agni, and those who have not, become intoxicated in the midst of Heaven, by svadhâ. With them, as a sovereign king, guiding life[1], adapt your body, as you wish.*

*10.18. 4 – I have placed this enclosure for the living. Let no one go there later, for whatever reason. Let them resurrect for a hundred full autumns and hide death with a mountain.*

Let us note, in passing, that these shlokas are taken from the 10th mandala. We will come back to this later.

# Sexuality

It is quite rare, in a study of a sacred book, to find a passage on sexuality. But, as we have just seen a little higher, the society was neither macho nor prudish. So, let us try to find out more.

One thing is certain: as we saw above about the statuettes, prudishness does not yet exist. Sexuality is not a taboo as it still is today. It does not seem to be a problem, neither for men nor for women.

In this shloka, Indranî – Indra's wife and/or his feminine aspect – speaks:

*10.86.6 – No woman has a more beautiful buttocks or is sexier than me. No one is more pleasant to squeeze, nor lifts her thighs as high as me. Indra is above all.*

Sexual metaphors are numerous. Here is one addressed to Soma Pavamana (purified).

*1.28.2 – There, where the two parts of the mortar are like two buttocks, Indra swallows the juice coming out of the mortar .*

Even the hymns to the Dawn contain them:

---
[1] Towards another life.

*1.123. 10 – In the triumph of grace, you go like a Young Woman, O Goddess, towards the god who approaches, desiring you. And, smiling Young Woman, you shine before him, revealing your breasts.*

*5.80.6 – She, the daughter of Heaven, turned towards men, lets her chest overflow, like a happy young girl, revealing her treasures to the pious. The young woman created the Light as before.*

As we have seen above, the Master of the House is married. He attends the sacrifice with his wife who drinks the soma just like him. But bigamy exists, at least among kings.

*7.18.2 – For, you truly dwell like a king with his wives, along the days in wisdom, O visionary. Sharpen the hymn in its preparation with Cows and Horses, for Wealth, for us who come to you.*

*7.18. 22 – Two hundred heads of cattle of the grandson of him who sings the gods, two chariots bring the women of Sudâsa. Deserving the gift of Pajavana[1], seated like the invoker around, I go away, celebrating it.*

*7.26.3 – He[2] made them, he will make others. Let the virtuous say it among the pressings. Like a husband alone with his wives, Indra has purified the cities in the same way, which is good for all.*

*8.2.42 – And he gave me his two granddaughters[3], full of the sap of pleasure, to be my wives.*

*1.105.8 – As two rival wives enclose the ribs on either side, they burn me. Cares devour me, I who sing to you, like a rat eating my rod, O Shatakratu. Heaven and Earth, understand my misfortune.*

*1.105.4 – Motionless in the assembly, the Mighty One sits between Heaven and Earth, the blessed one. The two Cows, co-wives, unharmed, not aging, are united*

---

[1] An ancestor of Sudâsa.
[2] Actions.
[3] Probably Heaven and Earth or Night and Dawn.

*in the pressing of the one who takes great strides¹.*

It seems that in the tenth mandala, which was added during the post-soma era, bigamy became more frequent, causing conflicts:

*10.145.1 – I dig this plant which grows the strongest with which she drives away co-wives, with which she keeps her husband.*

*10.145.2 – You, of beautiful appearance, produced by the gods, powerful, I blow away my co-wife. Let her make my husband solely mine.*

*10.159.6 – I have completely conquered them, I have conquered the co-wives, since I am the queen of my husband and of the people.*

Did sexual relations outside marriage exist? There are some clues to suggest so. When it comes to the husband, the word is *pati* which means husbond, but also lord, master. But from time to time the Rig Veda speaks of lover.

*1.152. 4 – We observe the lover² of the young women advancing and not falling dead, wearing a loose garment spreading around, the favorite abode of Mitra and Varuna.*

*3.33. 10 – (The Rivers speak) Yes, we listen to your words, O Artisan, you have come from afar with an imposing chariot, as the nursing woman bows before you, as the young girl opens herself to the man for you.*

*4.19. 7 – He caused the young virgins and unmarried women, knowing the truth, to flow like springs³. He watered the deserted plains. Indra satisfied their desires for a good husband.*

*9.32. 5 – The Cows rejoiced together as a young girl does with her lover, as if he were going to participate in a fight.*

---

[1] The Sun, or Vishnu.
[2] The Sun.
[3] Water gushing out.

And then there also seems to be a certain fantasy in sexual intercourse[4].

*10.101. 11 – The draft animal goes between the two masts, like one who has two women in his bed. Make the master of the forest stand in the wood. Place him at the bottom, without digging the source.*

In any case, these metaphors are numerous. While some are easily understandable, this is not the case for all of them.

*9.112. 4 – The Horse pulls[2] and stimulates her, the chariot rolls fast, the frog plays, the penis seeks the hairy slit. Flows around for Indra, O Indu.*

*8.1.34 – His thick member became visible, in front, hanging down along his thigh. His wife, seeing him, said: "O Noble One, you bring glorious food."*

*10.101. 12 – The penis, raise the penis, O Men. Stimulate it and copulate to gain Strength. Stimulate the son of Nishtigrî[3], for help. Stimulate Indra to drink the soma, here.*

Incest also exists, and does not seem to be well regarded by the gods. Let us note, however, that there is no authoritarian prohibition in the monotheistic manner.

*10.61.6 – When what was to be accomplished was in its midst, the lustful father made love to his young daughter. As they parted, they left a small stream that had sprinkled the back and into the womb.*

*10.10.7[4] – (Yamî speaks) The desire of Yama, my twin in the womb, has come to me to be together in the same bed. As a wife for her husband abandons her body, we could tear each other apart like the two wheels of a chariot.*

*10.10.8 – (Yama speaks) The spies of the gods who come here are not still. They do not close their eyes. With another than me, a lecher, goes quickly to tear you apart like two chariot wheels.*

---

[4] Let us not forget that India is the land of the Kama Sutra.
[2] ,Pull the cart or plow.
[3] Name of Indra's mother.
[4] This hymn is a dialogue between two twins, a boy and a girl.

Divorce also exists in this open-minded society, but it must not have been common, because there are not many allusions to it.

*10.95. 12 – (Purûravas) When will the son whom I have begotten desire his father? When will a tear roll down, like a wheel, recognizing me? When is a couple separated while the fire burns in the in-laws?*

## Alcohol:

Alcohol consumption also exists, but is not well regarded.

*8.2.12 – Drinkers who get drunk fight, as if they had alcohol in their hearts. They grow old like dried breasts.*

*7.86.6 – It is not one's own intelligence nor falsehood, O Varuna, but alcohol, stupidity, dice, heedlessness. The younger is a humiliation to the older. Surely sleep is not the one that expels error .*

*8.21. 14 – You know that no one can be rich to be a friend, those who drink alcohol insult you. When you make noise, when you push them, all together, you call them like a father.*

Alcohol, which is the drug of the West, stimulates violence. Fortunately, it must not have been common, because this is a resolutely peaceful society.

*8.114 – We have always considered ourselves calm and non-violent, and, suddenly, by your greatness, by your abundance, O Hero, we always rejoice in praise.*

*8.1.20 – I who always ask you with my hymn, desiring the soma, do not let me get angry like a wild tiger during the pressings. Who does not ask for power?*

Gambling is also a powerful addiction and is discouraged in hymn 10.34, here are some shlokas that speak about it.

*10.34.2 – She never got angry with me or got angry. She was kind to my friends and to me. I, because of a die, for the most important point, rejected the woman who loved me.*

*10.34.3 – My mother-in-law hated me, my wife rejected me: he who needs help, finds no one to show him compassion. "We have understood that a gambler is no more valuable than an old Horse."*

*10.34.6 – The player goes to the assembly, inflating his body, asking himself, will I win? The dice go against his desire, favoring the throws of his opponents.*

## Meat:

We saw that an animal was killed during sacrifices. It was eaten during or after the sacrifice.

*1.162.10 – When undigested food smokes from the belly and the smell of raw flesh, it is because the butcher has done his job well. Let them cook the meat well!*

*1.162.12 – Those who see the cooked Horse take it away and offer it to the gods, and those who ask for meat wait on the side for approval. Let us be served!*

*1.162.18 – The thirty-four ribs of the mighty swift Horse, parent of the gods, are cut off by the axe. Carefully cut the body, do it piece by piece, and recite aloud.*

But, in the tenth mandala we find this shloka which suggests that vegetarianism is not far away.

*10.28. 11 – The tendons have been torn from the foot, by those who revile the Brahmins, for their food. They eat whole reformed oxen, breaking the strength of their bodies themselves.*

## The Eunuchs

Eunuchs existed. They were even married. But we don't know much more about them.

*10.33.6 – They set out, desiring battle, against the army of the blameless Indra, encouraged by the Navagvas[1]. Like castrated eunuchs, they fled by the steep paths before Indra, the virile hero.*

*1.116.13 – In the great rite which was offered, O Nasatyas, you lords of many Riches, she called you, You heard the eunuch's wife as a command, and, O Ashvins, you gave her a son: Hiranyahasta[2].*

## Material Wealth

We saw in the first part of this work that it did not seem that a great inequality reigned between the members of this civilization. Of course, some were richer than others, that is how nature wants it. But enrichment was not the absolute priority as it is today.

*1.100. 9 – With his left hand he contains the powerful, with his right hand he holds together actions. He obtains Wealth even for the poor. May Indra and the Maruts be our protection.*

*4.25.7 – Indra is not friendly with the rich, nor with the miserly, nor with those who do not prepare soma. He loves the drinkers of soma. He presses for knowledge, and destroys dryness. He manifests Himself exclusively to the preparer of soma.*

## The sâdhus

---

[1] Literally "going by nine". Descendants of one of the first rishi: Angiras.
[2] Lit.: "golden hand".

The sâdhus, of the naga baba type – naked ascetic – make their appearance in the tenth mandala:

*10.136.1 – The hairy one carries the fire. The hairy one carries that which acts quickly[1]. The hairy one carries the Sky and the Earth. The hairy one carries the Sun which is seen by all. The hairy one is called Light.*

*10.136.2 – The ascetics, girded with wind, dress themselves in ashes[2], they follow the Force of the wind[3] when the gods have entered into them.*

They don't smoke chillum yet, but they drink bhang.

*10.136.7 – Vâyu crushed it for him, Kunannama crushed it[4] firmly when the hairy one drank what acts quickly with Rudra[5].*

---

[1] This is a drink. This word is usually translated as poison, venom, but here it seems to be Bhanga, a traditional Indian drink made from cannabis that ascetics are fond of.
[2] Ascetics, especially Naga Babas, cover themselves with ashes. The Sanskrit word malâ is usually translated as dust, dirt.
[3] They wander, unattached.
[4] The cannabis is crushed between two stones, and copiously watered with water, until it forms a sort of porridge which is mixed with milk, water and nowadays lassi.
[5] Rudra is the ancient name of the god Shiva, lord of Bhanga.

# The 7 Rivers Civilization

## Drought and soma shortage

As we saw when we studied the myths, droughts were not lacking in the long history of the Rig Veda. But the one that interests us now is that of 2,200 BCE.

This drought is well documented, probably because it is more recent and affected the entire intertropical zone, and above all, because it seriously disrupted several civilizations: the Egyptian empire, the Akkadian civilization in Mesopotamia and the Civilization of 7 Rivers, leading to population displacements.

*"The Indus Valley Civilization, which flourished in what is now Pakistan and northwestern India, was severely affected by this drought. Archaeological evidence suggests eastward migration and depopulation of major cities such as Mohenjo-daro and Harappa. Reduced rainfall would have led to diminished water resources and agricultural yields, destabilizing the economic foundations of the civilization."*
*(Pal et al., 2019, National Center for Biotechnology Information).*

It was part of a major climate disruption that would have lasted until 1,900 BCE and would have persisted between twenty years and a century according to studies, leading to a general cooling. It would have completed the desertification of the Sahara, which had already suffered a few millennia earlier, as we have seen in the myths.
The cooling and lack of rain has caused disruptions in the river system in the area we are studying.

*"Major rivers such as the Indus and its tributaries in Iran have seen their flows severely reduced, impacting irrigation and navigation, which are essential for trade and the survival of populations."*
*(Schuldenrein, 2008, Bioscience).*

Of course, drought also means lack of rain.

*"Regions of modern Iran, notably the Helmand Plain, also suffered the effects of this drought. Reduced rainfall affected crops and pastures, disrupting nomadic and agricultural lifestyles."*
*(Gangal et al., 2010, Vegetation History and Archaeobotany).*

This drought and disruptions generated migrations and reorganizations of societies.

*"The scarcity of resources forced populations to migrate to more fertile regions or to adapt to more arid conditions. This period is marked by significant social changes, including the reorganization of communities and the modification of economic structures."*
*(Staubwasser and Weiss, 2006, Quaternary International).*

The fauna and flora have obviously suffered from this situation.

*"The ecological disruption caused by this drought has caused imbalances in the fauna and flora, affecting the livelihoods of populations and forcing them to adapt their lifestyles."*
*(Weiss and Courty, 1993, Quaternary Research).*

Nevertheless, exports did not stop, as we saw in the first part. Good irrigation, thanks to the rivers, even weakened, limited the damage.

And then, if you don't have rain, you don't have mushrooms. It's as simple as that. So the soma ran out. Sure, it must have rained from time to time on mountain ranges like the Himalayas or the Hindukush, but it wasn't enough to produce enough mushrooms for this civilization, which had a population of at least five million.

Although not all the inhabitants drank soma, all the leaders of society and the wealthy families, that is, all those who had power, did so regularly, there was a serious shortage.
So they looked to replace the mushrooms with other plants.

*"Over the centuries, knowledge of the soma plant was completely lost, and Indian rituals reflect this, as in expiatory prayers that apologize to the gods for the*

*use of a substitute plant (such as rhubarb) due to the unavailability of Soma. By the time of the Brahmanas (800 BCE), additional substitutes for the plant mentioned in the Vedas had been discussed, including varieties of vines, herbs, and flowers."*
https://www.newworldencyclopedia.org/entry/Soma

*"Ayurvedic scholar Sushruta mentions 24 Soma plants, growing on the Himalayan lakes and named after Vedic meters. He also mentions 18 other Soma-like plants, which are mainly nerve herbs."*
https://www.vedanet.com/the-secret-of-the-soma-plant/

*"The Atharva Veda (AV XI.6.15) mentions five powerful plants of which Soma is the best, including marijuana, barley and darbha (kusha or durva), showing that many plants had qualities similar to Soma."*
https://www.vedanet.com/the-secret-of-the-soma-plant/

Soma grew in the mountains. It was harvested by peasants who sold it to a merchant. He put the plants to dry and went down to the plain to supply the sacrifices.

But the functioning of society required large quantities of mushrooms. Since they had almost disappeared, they used different plants without obtaining the same effects.

It is essential to take plants containing a molecule from the tryptamine family. And the substitute plants, even if, when they produce psychoactive effects, leave us in duality.

The most striking example is this mixture that archaeology has given us, finding in the Karakum civilization (Oasis civilization) during excavations in Turkmenistan by Viktor Sarianidi : ephedra, cannabis and poppy bud.

Poppy can be included in this mixture to calm the negative effects of the amphetamine-like alkaloids contained in ephedra.
The mixture of amphetamine and cannabis is well known. The effect is impressive and one can have powerful mystical experiences[1]. But we remain in duality,

---
[1] However, amphetamines are extremely dangerous products for health, and very addictive.

whereas with soma, there is no duality. It is non-duality.

"Psychedelic-induced experiences can sometimes closely resemble the most advanced forms of meditation and spiritual contemplation, particularly in their aspects of non-duality and dissolution of the sense of self."
Roland R. Griffiths, professor of psychiatry and behavior.

"Under the influence of psychedelic substances, people may experience a sense of merging with the universe, a heightened awareness of the spiritual dimension of existence, a disappearance of the sense of the individual self - phenomena similar to those encountered in Eastern contemplative traditions."
Huston Smith, philosopher and author specializing in religions.

"Research shows that psychedelics can allow access to non-dual and transpersonal states of consciousness, with a marked diminution of the sense of self and ego, comparable to that observed in experienced meditators."
Roland Griffiths, Department of Psychiatry and Behavior, Johns Hopkins University .

## The tenth mandala

The ninth mandala, which concluded the previous compilation, is entirely devoted to the soma, to the god Soma. It is the only one in the entire Rig Veda that is devoted to a single god. It contains hymns from all eras and all families of rishis. Like the eighth, it does not begin with a hymn to Agni.

The tenth, added after the shortage of soma, is composed, in part, of families of rishis unknown in the other mandalas. The vocabulary is also different. The words that are found only in this mandala are very numerous.

According to hymn 10.75, the one that lists the rivers, it was composed before the drying up of the Sarasvatî, which still flows, and after that of the Drishadvatî, which is not mentioned there.

**191 hymns**

The tenth mandala stands out sharply from the others. It contains 191 hymns, like the first mandala. Why this number? The definitive compilers of the Rig Veda did not choose this number at random. It must have a meaning, but what?

In this mandala, we see that a lot of information is included, as if the compilers wanted to add "technical" information on the society of the time.
Indeed, even though the hymns still speak of soma and sacrifices, we can see that they address many subjects that no longer have anything to do with spiritual practice: incest, gambling addiction, rivalry between co-wives, alcohol consumption, marriages, funerals, etc.

Why are these hymns which are intended to be sung, recited or murmured in sacrifices in this last mandala which was added well after the first nine?
What immediately comes to mind is that the Rig Veda is a collection intended to be passed down to future generations as civilization begins to decline.
We have seen that the Drishadvati no longer flows, but the Sarasvatî, yes, it still flows. The latter had two main tributaries: the Shutudrî – the Sutlej, today – and the Drishadvatî – the Chautang, today. The latter received the Yamuna, one of its

tributaries, which was diverted towards the East following an earthquake, as often happens in the Himalayas.
The Shutudrî, on the other hand, is still flowing. And it is still flowing today, but it became a tributary of the Indus following an earthquake. Its former bed has been identified by satellite[1].
So when Hymn 10.75 was written, which river was it flowing into? The Sarasvatî, or the Indus?

Geological studies in Pakistan have shown that the course of the Sutlej – the Shutudrî – was diverted between 1700 and 2000 BCE. It flowed into the Ghaggar – the Sarasvatî – before being diverted[2].

Since we have a demonstration that the hymn was composed towards the end of the Seven Rivers Civilization, before 1,900 BCE, we can assume that it was still flowing into the Ghaggar-Sarasvatî when the hymn was composed. Which is log ical, since it was the disappearance of the Sarasvatî's tributaries that dried it up. And since the Drishadvatî is not mentioned in the hymn to the rivers, only the Shutudrî – Sutlej – remained to feed it in addition to its smaller tributaries further north..

As for the drying up of the Drishadvati, we have only one quote before this last mandala. It is only directly mentioned in the third:

*3.33.4 – He has installed you in the enclosure of the Earth, in the seat of Ilâ, in the Light of days. O Agni, shine richly in Men, in the Drishadvatî and in the waves of the Sarasvatî .*

And indirectly in 1.152, the mandala which contains hymns from several eras. Between it and the Sarasvatî was the Brahmavarta – the country of Brahman – in which the battle of Kurukshetra would have taken place, that of the Mahâbhârata, a little later, it seems.

---

[1] See Michel Danino: On the trail of the lost river. Penguin books.
[2] Mughal, M. R. Ancient Cholistan. Archeology and Architecture. Rawalpindi-Lahore-Karachi: Ferozsons 1997, 2004.

*1.152.6 – May the Cows with smiling udders who favour Mamata, prosper in the country Avanti[1], who loves the mantra. May he, having drunk, share the Knowledge and call Aditi with a voice, and let wisdom escape from its exile.*

The third mandala is one of the oldest, even if it was not composed at the time when the events it describes took place. The hymn of the first is impossible to date, the temporal distance is far too large to give us a precise idea.

Let us now go to the Soma. Until before the addition of the 10th mandala, the compilation of the hymns of the Rig Veda ended with the ninth, entirely devoted to the god Soma, the deified drink. We have seen that the soma had a considerable importance for the proper functioning of society. It owes to it its pacifism and the peace that reigned for at least 1,500 years. And therefore, also, the prosperity that generally goes with peace.

We have also seen that the drought of 2,200 BCE lasted a long time, even a very long time, from ten years to a century, depending on the study. Such a long drought must have had consequences on the flora, particularly on fungi which need humidity.

Although it rained occasionally in the foothills of the Himalayas, the demand for mushrooms was enormous, since at that time the mature period was in full swing. The cities were very populated, trade was very flourishing despite the drought. Archaeologists have found no evidence of a decline in exports in Mesopotamia or elsewhere. Irrigation had replaced rain, as we have seen above.

There were therefore many householders. It was necessary to be able to supply them with soma, all together, on the dates fixed by the astronomers. The soma harvests were no longer sufficient.
The tenth mandala provides us with some clues that support this assertion. We have already seen them, they are the hymns that introduce an inequality among the four Varnas.
The Shudras become excluded from consuming soma in sacrifices[2].

---

[1] A region of Brahmavarta, the country between the Drishadvatî and the Sarasvatî.
[2] Which will continue during the classical Vedic period.

*10.90. 3 – His greatness is indeed great, but the Purusha is even greater. A quarter of him is composed of all the living; three-quarters of this immortal are in Heaven[1].*

*10.90.4 – Three-quarters have risen, one-quarter has returned here. He has walked towards everything that eats and everything that does not eat[2].*

And relatively quickly, the soma will disappear completely.

*10.85.3 – This one thinks he drank the soma, when they crushed the plant. But what the Brahmin knows, no one drinks, that is certain.*

*10.85.4 – Hidden by the arrangements of your guardians, O Soma, protected by them, you remain listening to the stones being pressed, no earthly one drinks you.*

Spiritual concerns will give way to others, much less elevated:

Greed will be one of the first. Hymn 10.107, of which here are some excerpts, demonstrates this perfectly:

*10.107.2 – Those who give gifts to the priests have risen into Heaven. Those who give Horses come with the Sun. Those who give gold receive immortality. Those who give clothes pass through life, O Soma.*

*10.107.3 – The gift to the priests is the divine reward. It is like a sacrifice to the gods and is surely not for the misers who do not bring it. However, many men bring it and present it, without fear.*

*10.107.5 – He who is rich in gifts is the first to be called. It is the village chief who walks in front. I think that he is the master of men, of peoples, since he is the first to make gifts.*

---

[1] First notion of inequality. A quarter of the population seems to be excluded from spirituality: the Shudras.
[2] Or the mobile and the immobile.

*10.107.7 – He gives the gift of Horse, the gift of Cow and when he gives gold, he gains the Light. He who loves us and knows it, makes the gift his own breastplate.*

The general situation is deteriorating, here is a shloka that alludes to it.

*10.28.4 – (Indra) Bear in mind, O Singer, that rivers flow in reverse, which is not possible. The fox turns against the lion, howling. The jackal rushes upon the wild boar, driving it out of the thickets.*

The fear of death takes on great importance, as we can see in this hymn to Soma.

*10.18.1 – Go far away, Death, by the other way than that which leads to the gods. I say to him who sees and hears: do not harm my descendants, nor my heroes.*

*10.59.4 – Do not deliver us to death, O Soma. May we see, now, the Sun rise. With the days, may our old age be comfortable and drive away destruction, as far as possible.*

Until then, soma gave immortality, and now in this hymn the rishi asks Soma not to deliver him to death... Times are changing...

The political functioning of society is changing and so is the role of the king.

*10.173. 1 – You have come here. Be in the middle, stand firmly, firmly. Let all the people desire you. Let your kingship[1] not fail.*

However, the beginnings of democracy, as we understand it today, seem to exist:

*10.124.8 – They unite with the best that pleases Indra. It resides by its own nature in those who get drunk. They have it chosen as a people chooses its king. They kept themselves, prudently, apart from Vritra.*

---

[1] The word Râja, which is usually translated as king, is misleading. The root means: to reign, to administer, to manage, to represent and can be appropriate for a monarch as well as a simple mayor. The Varnas, which we have seen in hymn 10.90, cite the Râjanyas as the second "caste" and not kshatriyas, which will become the official name of this Varna, whose root means "domination, supremacy".

But, not everything is negative. The society, which functions very well at the economic level, has organized itself and is preparing for the future through development and, probably, the organization of education:

*10.32.7 – Since he who does not know the field has asked him who knows it, he goes on his way, instructed by him who knows the field. This is, indeed, the benefit of instruction, because he has found the way that leads straight ahead.*

The belief in reincarnation becomes clearer :

*10.5. 7 – The non-existent and the existent are in Heaven, the farthest, at the birth of the efficacious Aditi. For Agni is the first-born of Truth: Bull and Cow in his previous lives.*

The practice of austerities seems to be born, or to develop clearly. The seals found in the ruins, during the excavations, show us characters sitting in a yoga position, the two soles of the feet, stuck to each other, while keeping the body straight. It is very difficult to achieve. This type of posture is practiced during austerities that the yogi inflicts on himself, to elevate his spirit.

*10.109.1 – We were the first to speak of the offence against the Brahmans . Mâtarishvan is a boundless ocean. Bringing austerities, the mighty divine Waters, rejoicing, are the first-born by the Truth.*

*10.109.4 – The ancient gods and the first seven rishis, in full austerity, spoke of it: "The wife of the brahmin is terrifying when she is disturbed, when one approaches her. She must be placed further away, in Heaven."*

*10.154.2 – Those have become invincible through austerity. Through austerity, they have gone to Heaven. They have made austerity their greatness. For them, then let him depart!*

We know that the Upanishads are not yet composed, but we see positive morality appearing:

*10.117.2 – He who has food, when a weak and miserable person approaches, desiring to eat, closes his mind even if they have known each other for a long time, will find no one to help him.*

*10.117.3 – This one is a hospitable one. He gives to the beggar who wanders, weakened, desiring food. He easily becomes the one who responds to his request for help and later becomes his friend.*

*10.117.5 – He who is stronger should give to the one who suffers. He should see along the way, for Riches turn like the wheels of a chariot, and go from one to another.*

With soma having almost disappeared, or having been replaced by other ineffective plants, hymns that speak of something other than Enlightenment are multiplying:

An hymn against miscarriage:

*10.162.1 – With a mantra, let Agni the demon-slayer drive away from here this disease, with the wrong name, which is in your fetus, which remains in your womb.*

Against diseases:

*10.163.1 – From your eyes, from your nose, from your ears, from your chin, from your brain which is in your head, from your tongue, I extract the disease from you.*

Against nightmares:

*10.164. 3 – When, through desire, through weakness, through imprecation, we have been foolish, awake or asleep, let Agni chase away, far away, everything that hurts us or saddens us.*

*10.164.6 – We have conquered today. We have won: we have become without stupidity. Let the daydream, the bad manners go to those who hate us, let them go to those who detest us.*

For the birth of a son:

*10.183.2 – (The husband) I have seen you, with my reflective mind, in your search for help during your menstruation, in your body. Near me, the woman has become superior. Generate a birth, you who want a son.*

To get pregnant:

*10.184.1 – May Vishnu prepare the womb. May Tvashtri carve the forms. May Prajapati pour it[1]. May the creator place the fetus in you.*

To these hymns we can add those which we have seen in the chapters devoted to manners and morality.
These hymns of the 10th mandala show us clearly that the era is no longer the same, and that sacrifices were no longer solely focused on high spirituality.

---

[1] Pour the sperm.

We also find what exists in every culture: the creation of the material world:

*10.129. 1 – The non-existent did not exist. The existent did not exist, at that moment. There was neither the Intermediate World nor the Heaven. Who turned? Where was the protection? What Waters were impenetrable and deep?*

*10.129.2 – Death did not exist. Immortality did not exist, at that time. There was no form of night or day. He[1] breathed, without wind, by his own will. Surely there was nothing else, beyond that.*

*10.129.3 – Darkness existed, hidden by Darkness, in the beginning. All of it existed, without distinction, unstable. All of it existed? Void was hidden by void. Only one was born by the greatness of heat.*

But this hymn does not tell a legend, it ends with questions:

*10.129. 6 – Who really knows? Who will proclaim it here? Why this birth? Why this creation? The gods are after it. So, who knows where it comes from?*

*10.129.7 – How did this creation come into being? Was it realized or was it not? He who, in the farthest Heaven, observes this world, surely knows. And what if he did not know?*

And the Rig Veda ends with a hymn to the Union.

*10.191.1 – O Agni, you unite, closely, all the Âryas. Bring us all the Riches when you are inflamed, on the path[2].*

*10.191.2 – Come together. Speak together. Know by your minds, since the ancient gods know the portion[3] and worship it.*

*10.191.3 – Common is the mantra. Common is the assembly. Common is their thought through their mind. I declare to you what unites us and that I practice sacrifice.*

---

[1] The Brahman.
[2] On the path to enlightenment.
[3] Portion of spiritual wealth, enlightenment.

## The 7 Rivers Civilization

*10.191.4 – Common is our desire. Common are our hearts. Let your thought be common so that you may truly be together.*

Obviously, this is a hymn addressed to the population of the time or perhaps to the descendants for whom this latest compilation is intended.

And here we come to a point that has never really been addressed: why did they make this last compilation, that is to say, add the tenth mandala at the end of civilization?

Yes, okay, the Sarasvatî is still flowing well. But since the Drishadvati is dry, its flow is still much less powerful.
On the other hand, the monsoon that has been unregulated for several decades does not encourage optimism. And then, also, the Sarasvatî is a goddess. The only river that is. It is also on its banks that the confederation of the Pûrus lived[1]. It is from this confederation of families that the Bharatas came.
So, seeing their goddess decline must have probably encouraged some Brahmins to introduce to new generations what this civilization was, which had a taste of the Golden Age.

---

[1] 7.96

# Concrete functioning of the society

# The castes

Ah!, here is a subject that ignites ethnocentric Westerners[1]. This word, of Portuguese origin, indistinctly groups two things: the Varnas and the Jâtis. Varna means color, and Jâti life. The Varnas come from the Rig Veda and the Jâtis arrived much later. Starting from the Varnas, these subdivisions have transformed over the millennia into sorts of guilds or corporations. You have Jâtis of taxi drivers, tea carriers, and even thieves or prostitutes.... These Jâtis also serve as social service.

The Varnas are something else. First, these castes appear only in the tenth mandala, that is, in the mature period, because the Rig Veda does not speak of them at all in the first nine mandalas. At most, we find from time to time the word Brahmana, which designates the priests[2]. But that is all. The words: Râjanya, Vaishya and Shûdra did not yet exist.

For a Vedic Indian, society is composed of four colours. It is in four-color process. But Varna does not mean contempt, division or intolerance. In the Rig Veda, nothing says that castes are closed, excessively hierarchical, nor that they generate contempt or hatred.
People could change their Varnas according to their social status. For example, a Shudra who decides to start a labor business, must become a Vaishya, since he is an entrepreneur.
The same is true for a Vaishya who becomes bankrupt and is forced to seek employment. He becomes a Shudra.

---

[1] **Ethnocentrism:** Tendency to favor the ethnic group to which one belongs and to make it the only model of reference.
[2] And also the shlokas or mantras.

Even today, any person, regardless of his social status, even the untouchables[1], or a mleccha[2], like me, can become a Brahmin, if he knows the Veda.

The society of that time had greatly simplified the life of these people thanks to the Varnas.

**The Brahmanas** : As we have seen above, the root of this word means to grow, to make grow. Their duty was to grow spiritually, themselves, and to make the rest of society grow. Some of them could be priests, but not all of them. Others could be gurus, or for the Masters of the House, be the Purohita, the equivalent of chaplains in the Middle Ages, in our western countries.
Others could live as more or less ascetics. What really mattered was to attain En lightenment, for themselves, and for others.

**The Râjanyas** : These are the leaders. This caste will change its name after the Rig Veda and will become Kshatriya. The roots are totally different and thus demonstrate that there was a very strong change in mentality after the Rig Veda. Râjanya is a word based on the root *râj* which means to rule, represent, administer, manage. We translate it as king, but it could also be translated as mayor or burgomaster.

Kshatriya comes from the root *kṣatra*, which means domination, supremacy. And the word kshatriya is usually translated as warrior. Indra is referred to as a Kshatriya more than once.

*1.81. 2 – You are a hero, you are a warrior, you are the great Distributor, you make the weak grow, you help the priests of sacrifice by giving them much Wealth.*

*6.18.2 – He, the mighty warrior, causing tumult, always on the same road, the one who hurts a lot, who loudly honors the juice of the third pressing that moves in the vast dust of men, has become an ordinary human.*

This difference in words, and therefore in meaning, went almost unnoticed by the French translators who translated Râjanya as warrior and even as Kshatriya!!!

---
[1] Who do not exist in the Rig Veda.
[2] A barbarian.

This is a fundamental difference, because there is nothing to say that the Râ-janyas were violent, domineering and authoritarian. As we have seen in the first part of this work, there are no palaces, no statues or warlike frescoes.
Their role in society is to lead it. Leaders can only come from that caste whose members were trained for their future duty.

**The Vaishyas** : This word comes from the root *viś*, which means community, people; tribe. They are the entrepreneurs, the artisans, the traders, the farmers.... Their role in society is economic. Some may be very rich, others poor. The rich, the Masters of the House, had to offer sacrifices and therefore drink the soma. The poor, having no power, were not required to do so.

**The Shudra** : the root *śudh* means pure. They are the proletarians. Today, they would be called wage earners, employees. They are all those who have only their arms to live on.

Material wealth does not intervene in these Varnas. A Brahmin can be a beggar, and a Shudra can be a billionaire. It does not matter, but both will have to drink the soma. The Brahmin, because he has to take care of growing the spirit and the Shudra because he has become rich and therefore powerful.

The average Westerner, when he hears the word caste, understands: inequality of rights.

Now, it is not a question of rights, but of duties. And those who have the strictest duties are, quite logically, the "higher" castes. This is the natural consequence of the sacrifices. The members of these castes have a responsibility of capital importance: to manage society well, in the interest of all. And for this, it was imperative, for the two higher castes, the Brahmanas and the Râjanyas, as well as for the rich Vaishyas, to drink the soma in the sacrifices and consequently to seriously diminish their ego.

The Shudras, the proletarians, were not required to do so. They could do so, but since they were generally not rich, they had no power. And so, whether they had an ego or not had no consequences for society. On the other hand, if they became masters of a house, and therefore had power, then they had to offer sacrifices and drink soma. And also change caste.

*10.90.3 – His greatness is indeed great, but the Purusha[1] is even greater. One-fourth of him is composed of all the living; three-fourths of this immortal are in Heaven.*

*10.90.4 – Three-quarters have risen, one-quarter has returned here. He has walked towards everything that eats and everything that does not eat[2].*

*10.90.11 – When they fixed the Purusha, into how many parts did they condition him? Who was his face? Who were his two arms? Who were his thighs? Who were his feet? Say!*

*10.90.12 – The Brahmanas were the face. The Râjanyas were made by his two arms. As for his thighs, they were the Vaishyas. The Shudras were born as feet.*

This society functioned very well as long as soma was abundant. But when soma ran out, the egos came back, slowly, of course, but within two or three generations, the mentality began to change.

Some of the priests will make the perfect accomplishment of the sacrifice the indispensable condition to obtain what is asked of the gods. The soma will be replaced by other more or less psychoactive plants. These priests will assert their power.

Other priests will turn to the Upanishads and develop other techniques to achieve enlightenment, such as certain yoga asanas, pranayama, meditation etc....

They are the ones who will create Hinduism.

---

[1] Humanity, or even society.
[2] Or the mobile and the immobile.

# The opposition and its arguments

Of course, all of the above is violently contested by the proponents of the famous invasion-migration.

When we discuss with them, they refute our arguments, often with a certain verbal violence. They support, tooth and nail, this arrival of Aryans in the middle of the second millennium BCE. But, they are all unable to cite a single hymn speaking of an arrival of population, of a new country, of a country that is regretted etc.

Only a few writers[1] cite in their endnotes a few hymns speaking of battles. But never of invasion-migration.

# The horses

The main argument in past years was that India did not have wild horses on its soil.
While it is true that the Thar Desert has little in common with the plains of the Far West, there were horses in Iran, Afghanistan and Turkmenistan, countries with which the Seven Rivers Civilization had trading posts and commercial and cultural relations from the beginning.

*The Akhal-Teké horse is a breed famous for its beauty, endurance and resistance to harsh climatic conditions. Originating from Turkmenistan, this horse was used by nomadic tribes for raids and long-distance races.*
*DP Sponenberg, The Prolific and Enduring Akhal-Teke Horse, Journal of Animal Breeding and Genetics, 2015.*

---

[1] Notably David Reich in his book "Who We Are and How We Got There". ed. Quanto 2019, and David W. Anthony and al., "The horse, the wheel, and language: how Bronze-Age riders from the Eurasian steppes shaped the modern world", Princeton University Press, 2010.

*Akhal-Teké are known for their unique metallic coat that gives them an almost shimmering appearance in the sun. This characteristic is due to the particular structure of their hair."*
LK Harris, The Shimmering Beauty of Akhal-Teke Horses, Equine Science Review, 2018.

*Statuette found in Harappa*

*Nisaen horses, originating from ancient Persia (present-day Iran), were renowned in ancient times for their speed and elegance. They were often reserved for kings and nobles, symbolizing power and wealth.*
P. Crawford, Nisean Horses of Ancient Persia, Historical Equine Studies, 2013.

*The Nisaen was particularly prized by Persian warriors for its ability to cover long distances without tiring, making it a valuable asset for military campaigns.*
AR Bell, The Role of Nisean Horses in Persian Warfare, Journal of Ancient Military History, 2017.

The Afghan horse was found in the north of the country, right next to the settlement of Shortugai, in the Oxus civilization, also called Bactria-Margiana. The ancients spoke a lot about it.

*"The horses of Afghanistan, especially those of Bactria, are renowned for their vigor and beauty. Herodotus, the Greek historian, mentions the presence of these horses in the Persian armies, testifying to their importance in ancient civilizations." – Herodotus, Histories.*

*"Bactrian horses, bred from the fertile plains of ancient Afghanistan, were prized not only for their endurance but also for their ability to traverse the most difficult*

*terrain, making them the mounts of choice for armies and messengers." – Quintus Curtius Rufus, Histories of Alexander the Great*

*"The Afghan horsemen, mounted on their powerful horses, were feared on the battlefields of antiquity. These horses, carefully bred in the Bactrian steppes, symbolized strength and freedom" – Arrian, Anabasis of Alexander.*

Even if a shloka reminds us of wild horses in India, it is more likely that it speaks to us of Afghanistan, Turkmenistan or Iran.

*10.79.7 – Born in the woods, horses, coming from everywhere, are caught with ropes thrown. This friend who is well-born, with the Vasus, has cut off the joints that make one grow and prosper.*

The horses seem numerous, and caught with a lasso. But was it on the other side of the Kyber-Pass or in the north of Iran, with the Caspian horse, ancestor of the Arabian horse?
Trade and commerce certainly contributed to supplying horses to the Seven Rivers Civilization.

# Linguistic

The linguistic argument has not changed since the 19th century. Here are the main ones:

- The Indo-European language family shows strong similarities with Sanskrit and the Indo-Iranian languages, suggesting a common origin.
- The Vedic texts refer to conquering "arya" peoples who came from the northwest.
- Some Sanskrit words have no equivalents in the Dravidian languages, indicating an external influence.
- There are marked linguistic differences between North and South India.

That there are many points in common between Sanskrit and the European languages, no one seriously disputes. We find in each of them many common roots,

---
[1] This shloka is about the sacrificed beast. Which was rare and will be abandoned later.

vocabulary as well as points of grammar. This is particularly evident in the Celtic languages (the dual[1] in Breton, for example).

On the other hand, the Vedic texts never say that the Aryas were conquerors and even less that they came from the North-West. This is pure fiction.

That there is a difference between the Dravidian and Sanskrit languages seems quite logical. India was not populated in one go. Neither were other countries. No country was populated in one go.

The **Out of India Theory** is the opposite theory. It says that European languages came from India. Is this more implausible than the unofficial invasion-migration theory?

This invasion was born in the mind of a great German Sanskritist living in England: Friedrich Max Müller, translator of the Rig Veda in the 19th century, in the middle of the colonial period. This was the time when scientists, totally ethnocentric, saw the West bringing civilization to other peoples whom they considered as barely human savages.

The Out of India Theory, developed by Shrikant Talageri[2] and others, takes a different perspective. According to this theory, the five Vedic peoples mentioned in the Rig Veda migrated from East to West. Starting from the Sarasvatî region, they crossed what is now Pakistan and then settled in Afghanistan. This hypothesis is supported by architectural evidence such as the settlement of Shortugai in northern Afghanistan, which supplied the Seven Rivers Civilization with copper and tin, which were needed for the production of bronze.

From there, these peoples would have gone up through the territories corresponding today to Tajikistan, Turkmenistan and Uzbekistan, before gradually establishing themselves on the plains of Eurasia.

So who is right? Who is wrong?

---

[1] Or what's left of it.
[2] Rig Veda, an historical analysis. Aditya Prakashan Edition. 2000.

There is another possibility that we have explored by studying the myths: the great drought of 6200 BCE, accompanied by a general cooling of the northern hemisphere. This period of drought and cooling was caused by intense volcanic activity. As a result, many population movements occurred towards the equator.

The Myth of Shushna could be an alternative theory. On the other hand, the hymns that speak of it cannot date from this period: spoked wheels had not yet been invented. Nor were copper weapons.

# Genetics

Of course, genetics is involved. Studies on population movements and the settlement of the Earth are multiplying. Western geneticists, such as David Reich, for example, are publishing studies that have mobilized many researchers and large financial resources.

According to David Reich, in his book "Who We are, and How We Got There" Quanto editions 2008, Europe and India were populated by the Yamnayas, a Ukrainian tribe, around 5,000 years ago for Europe and between 1,000 and 2,000 BCE for India.

This claim is based on their Y chromosome – the father's DNA – which is found all over Europe. It is, curiously, in very high proportion among peoples living further west, near the sea, such as the Bretons who are Celts, while this proportion is lower inland.

He claims that this Y chromosome is found in the inhabitants of the area we are studying: northwest India, who speak an Indo-European language.
But he couldn't go into detail because, he said, fossil DNA is not preserved in West Asia.

*"Y chromosome studies show that haplogroups R1a, frequently associated with Yamnaya steppe populations, are significantly present in Indo-European populations in India, suggesting significant migration and genetic influence of these peoples in the region."*

*Peter A. Underhill et al., The phylogenetic and geographic structure of Y-chromosome haplogroup R1a. European Journal of Human Genetics, 2015.*

*"Analysis of genetic markers on the Y chromosome indicates a migration of the Yamnayas to India that would have taken place around 3,500 to 4,000 years ago, bringing with them genetic characteristics that are still observable today."*
*David W. Anthony et al., The horse, the wheel, and language: how Bronze-Age riders from the Eurasian steppes shaped the modern world, Princeton University Press, 2010.*

These Yamnayas, before settling in Ukraine, lived in the Caucasus. And like everyone else, they came from Africa[1]. Now the Caucasus is located between the Black Sea and the Caspian Sea, just above Iran and very close to Turkmenistan and Afghanistan. Does their Y chromosome date from this period or was it born in Ukraine?
On the other hand, David Reich begins his chapter on the settlement of India by saying that the Rig Veda tells of the invasion of India by Aryan warriors and he gives the numbers of the hymns that prove this: 1.33; 1.53; 2.12; 3.30; 3.34; 4.16; 4.28.

As you can verify for yourselves in my translation, or those of other translators, you will notice that these hymns speak of war, but not of black-skinned people[2], and not at all of migration, nor of invasion, nor of displacement of population, nor of a country that one regrets, nor anything that suggests an invasion-migration.

And then there are other analyses: those done on mitochondrial DNA – the mother's DNA – which is more difficult to analyze.
It proves the opposite. Studies show that female populations have not undergone significant migrations and that Indian women have largely contributed to the current genetic pool of India.

---

[1] In the current state of our knowledge.
[2] These words appear only twice in the entire Rig Veda, but not in the hymns it quotes. They appear in 1.130.8 and in 9.41.1.

*"Mitochondrial DNA analyses show deep genetic continuity among Indian populations, going back tens of thousands of years, suggesting that male migrations did not have the same impact on maternal lineages."*
Toomas Kivisild et al., *"The Genetic Heritage of the Earliest Settlers Persists Both in Indian Tribal and Caste Populations, American Journal of Human Genetics, 2003.*

*"Mitochondrial DNA studies indicate that maternal lineages in India have remained relatively stable and homogeneous over millennia, despite male migrations detected by Y chromosome analyses."*
Sanghamitra Sengupta et al., *"Polarity and Temporality of High-Resolution Y-Chromosome Distributions in India Identify Both Indigenous and Exogenous Expansions and Reveal Minor Genetic Influence of Central Asian Pastoralists,"* *American Journal of Human Genetics, 2006.

*"While the paternal lineages show signs of Indo-European migrations, the maternal lineages, analyzed through mitochondrial DNA, demonstrate marked stability, reflecting a complex settlement pattern with predominant indigenous influence."*
Kumarasamy Thangaraj et al., *"Reconstructing the Origin of Andaman Islanders, Science, 2005.*

Weird, isn't it? Don't you think? The women are supposedly from India, and the men are warriors from the Eurasian steppes?

Let's summarize the two opinions. Let's start with the dominant theory:

1- Y-DNA haplogroups: Analyses of Y-chromosome haplogroups show a strong presence of haplogroups R1a, particularly R1a1a, which are often associated with the peoples of the Indo-European steppes.

2- Indo-European Migrations: It is assumed that these men belonged to the Indo-European populations who moved south from the steppes of Central Asia, bringing with them their language and culture.

3- Patrilineality[1]: Historical Indo-European societies were often patrilineal, which could explain why the male genetic impact is more visible in Y lineages.

The last two points are guesses. Now let's look at the other DNA:

1- Diversity of MT-DNA Haplogroups: Analyses show a high diversity of mitochondrial haplogroups, suggesting older continuity and genetic diversity in female populations of North India.
2- Local continuity: Some studies indicate that the mitochondrial DNA of current populations of North India has deep and ancient roots in the region, before the migrations from the steppes.
3- Endogamous Marriages: Social practices such as endogamous marriages (within the same community or caste) were able to maintain and diversify maternal lineages, contributing to a rich genetic mosaic.

The last point is a guess. A solid guess, nonetheless, because endogamy is still strictly practiced in India via castes (Jâtis), which delights Bollywood producers. But castes have only existed since the end of the mature period. What about before? Nothing in the first nine mandalas suggests that there was a separation, a compartmentalization between different parts of the population of the pre-urban era. For that, we will have to wait for the tenth mandala. The one that was added when the Sarasvatî was still flowing but the Drishadvatî had already dried up.

The famous steppe migration(s), or the former Aryan invasion, are thought to have taken place during the second millennium BCE. They may have left genetic traces, but absolutely no archaeological traces.
In fact, the very numerous excavations carried out in both Pakistan and India have not found the slightest proof of this migration, which geneticists no longer set at 1500 BCE but, more cautiously, "during the second millennium".
No pottery suggesting the massive arrival of another culture. No weapons of war.... nothing. Absolutely nothing!

---

[1] Said of a mode of filiation for which only paternal kinship counts. (The name, privileges, membership in a clan or class are transmitted from the father and the father's parents to the children; no rights are recognized to the parents on the maternal side.) Larousse.

Unless, of course, this migration did not take place at that time, but much earlier: in 6200 BCE during the great drought and cooling of the northern hemisphere, which was the cause of many population movements, from north to south.
Which doesn't explain why the DNA of Indian men was replaced by that of the arrivals. Unless there was a genocide targeted at men. Which seems big anyway.

So we will have to wait for further information before being affirmative.

And then there is another thing that no one talks about: migration by sea. When you have a good command of navigation, based on the stars, it is much simpler and safer to travel by sea than by land, where there are many unpleasant surprises, whether due to nature or humans.
Obviously, this possibility only concerns the Out of India Theory. The Caspian Sea and the Black Sea are automatically eliminated.

## After 1900 BCE

We have seen that the 7 Rivers Civilization ended around 1900 BCE except in Gujarat where it continued for about 5 centuries.

It ended following the drying up of Sarasvatî, following an earthquake, in a context of climatic changes and unregulated monsoons.
It is also quite possible that the firing of millions of bricks, used to build cities, had a significant impact on the environment.

Of course, the population did not disappear. It did not fly away. Some stayed put, adopting a rural life. Others, much more numerous, left for the Ganges plain. Still others left for the North and others for the West via Iran. This is what archaeologists call the post-Harappan phase. The sites are numerous and well excavated. The cultural continuity, from Vedism to Hinduism is evident: swastikas, pipal leaves[1] on artifacts, yoga, weights and measures, craft techniques, boats, symbolism, checkerboard games, etc.

The sacrifices continued. The soma was no longer the same, but the ritual did not change. To replace the soma, ephedra mixed with cannabis was used, as in other small civilizations such as that of the Oxus, the Oases and Zoroastrianism. The effect was not the same. Ephedra, even mixed with cannabis, does not allow one to know non-duality. Its active principle is that of amphetamines and is not a tryptamine. It therefore does not help to obtain enlightenment. On the other hand, the experience can be extremely impressive, but there is always duality. And when there is duality, you are always in the Intermediate World, not yet in Heaven.

To remedy this, some of the priests developed, in the course of the Upanishads, other techniques to obtain it, such as yoga, meditation, pranayama. On the other hand, the Ego of the leaders returned with the consequences that it entails and the classical Vedic civilization was born gradually.

---

[1] Pagoda fig tree.

# Politics

If in the West, the prehistory of India leaves almost everyone indifferent, it is not the same in India. The main subject, which divides Indian society, is the famous Aryan invasion, which is said to have taken place in 1,500 BC (or 1,500 BCE). It was the British who brought this idea, following one of the first translations of the Rig Veda.

The intellectuals of the time noted that the Indians had many more very ancient books than the Christian Westerners. Vexed, they interpreted some passages of the Rig Veda, as irrefutable proof that the language and the whole Indian culture had been brought by a people of warriors, white with blue eyes, who came from Europe. They would have been superior, by strength and intelligence, to the Indians with black skin, therefore half savage.

Since India's independence, a large number of Western-trained Indian scientists have looked into the problem and begun to challenge this colonialist and racist vision of the settlement of India.

The discovery of Harappa in 1910 changed everything. Not immediately, of course, but gradually, because the British view had been adopted by many of them: the Dravidian militants, some upper castes and some light-skinned people in northern India.

So, very logically, politics got involved, at both national and international levels.

Internationally: Most of the so-called Indus civilization is in Pakistan, which is an Islamic republic that is angry with the Indian republic, which is, theoretically, religiously neutral. Pakistan will never accept that the ruins of this civilization have anything to do with Vedism. Nearly or far.

At the national level: opinions are very divided, political recoveries are numerous and from all sides. From the left to the right, passing through all political nuances, this invasion is the subject of multiple controversies in which I refuse to enter.

I have often been criticized by Westerners, who have never read the Rig Veda, for supporting this or that Indian political party. So, I want to clarify that I am absolutely not interested in the Indian nation-state, which the British created in 1947, leaving, against their will, at the time of independence. No more than I am interested in the Pakistani nation-state, created in the same way, at the same time.

What interests me is the truth. Nothing else.

# Proposal of a history

The history I am offering you can only be assumed. Nothing, or almost nothing, is tangible evidence, demonstrated by renowned scientists apart from the dates of the eclipse and the drying up of Sarasvatî.

1- Around 6200 BCE:

A major drought struck the entire northern hemisphere in 6200 BCE. This drought was accompanied by a general cooling of this hemisphere, leading to many population movements.

It is possible that the myth of Shushna, who arrives at the head of an army, is described in this climatic episode and that it could tell of the arrival of new peoples in India.
This myth does not mention the black-skinned Dasyus. So I do not think that these are the famous "Aryans" that the scholars of the 19th century liked so much.

2 – Around 5300 BCE.

This date corresponds to the eruption of a super-volcano, off the coast of Japan. According to volcanologists, it would be the largest volcanic eruption in the entire history of humanity, which had dramatic consequences on the climate and populations. It could correspond to the myth of Vritra, the one who holds back the waters, who blocks the rivers – the rain – while making an enormous cloud, hiding the Light of the Sun. It does not speak of Dasyus, nor of black skin either.

3 – Approximately between 5,300 and 3,500 BCE

Here we will enter into History, very roughly all the same. The king of the Bharatas, Divodâsa, fights the Dâsa Shambara and destroys his ninety-nine strongholds.

Divodâsa – the servant of heaven – is the grandfather of Sudâsa who will win the war of the ten kings, less than a century later.
Unfortunately, we lack the information to have a more precise date.
It seems that the aggressors were Shambara and his Dasas. It seems obvious that Shambara was well established in the country of the seven rivers, since he had at least ninety-nine strongholds, even if this number is not necessarily to be taken literally.
On the other hand, the black-skinned Dasyus do not appear in these hymns.

4 – About a century after the previous date.

Divodasa's battles with Shambara are now only a memory. The five basic Vedic peoples are clearly identified. Sudâsa, the grandson of Divodâsa, king of the Bharatas, also faces a revolt of all the other peoples, including the Pûrus, from whom the Bharatas are descended. These five Vedic peoples unite with five non-Vedic peoples. Sudâsa, a Tritsu - a branch of the Bharatas - fights them in a murderous war on the Parushnî and the Yamuna.

Then all these peoples reconcile, according to the rule that we have already seen and which will be described in the laws of Manu, much later.
The first compilation of the Rig Veda – mandalas 2 to 7 – sealed the peace agreements between the Vedic peoples.
This war left its mark on people's minds and seems to be at the origin of the peaceful period. The consumption of soma most likely contributed to this.

5 – Around 3,500 BCE.

Cities are emerging from the Earth. Spirituality is perfectly regulated and peaceful and non-violent life has become the rule. Another compilation of the Rig Veda will be made over the centuries. Mandalas 1, 8 and 9 will be added.

6 – Around 2,600 BCE.

The mature phase of civilization does not begin everywhere at the same time, from an archaeological point of view. But the economy is working at full capacity. Exports are breaking records. The population seems happy and fulfilled. The Rig Veda, with its nine mandalas, is THE sacred book, oral of course, of this period.

7 – Around 2,200 BCE.

A severe drought causes a shortage of soma. As the rains no longer fall over the entire intertropical strip, the mushrooms cannot withstand it. The priests turn to other plants, notably ephedra mixed with cannabis and also the blue lotus.
But these plants are not entheogenic, even if the effects can be impressive, the result does not follow.

Little by little, the ego returns with its harmful, but still embryonic, consequences.
The climate is changing. Monsoons are no longer regular. This does not affect international trade, because water still flows relatively abundantly in the rivers.

The thoughts of the population are less oriented towards spirituality. The hymns evoke concerns that have little to do with the search for enlightenment.

8 – Between 2,000 and 1,900 BCE.

Several earthquakes divert the courses of the two major tributaries of the Sarasvatî: the Yamuna[1] and the Shutudrî – the Sutlej, today. The tenth mandala is added. The end of civilization is looming. A large part of the population based on the Sarasvatî moves to the banks of the Indus.

9 – From 1,900 to 1,400.

Almost the entire population left, with the exception of that of Gujarat, which would continue for five centuries longer than the others.
A good part will settle in the Ganges plain. Others will go to the West, still others will go to the North, towards the Eurasian plains.
Concrete and practical spirituality, thanks to soma, will be transformed into religion. The Veda will give way, over the centuries, to Vedanta, and to Hinduism.

---

[1] The Yamuna flowed into the Drishadvatî – the Chautang today.

# Conclusion

The Seven Rivers Civilization was therefore a totally atypical civilization. As we have just seen, no other civilization of this importance and of this kind has existed to my knowledge. The first small civilizations or city-states must have had a similar functioning, as demonstrated by excavations in Turkmenistan, Afghanistan, Iran and Pakistan[1], but not the other important civilizations.

A million square kilometers in size, its main characteristics have never been taken up by other civilizations: total pacifism, non-centralization of power and the practice of sacrifices with the consumption of a psychedelic.

The Seven Rivers Civilization was also ahead of its time in urban planning, where comfort was accessible to all, rich or poor. Its water management system could have been the stuff of dreams for many other civilizations of that time, and those that followed.

The low social inequality, the absence of displays of luxury and glorification of individuals were due to the consumption of soma as part of a spiritual approach. Its main property is to dissolve the ego, and therefore, at the same time, to make greed, aggression and violence disappear among the elites of society. The community-type functioning, instead of pitting the inhabitants against each other, allowed a form of democracy, which has little to do with the one we know today and which is really democratic only in name.

Their spirituality, concrete and practical, took place outside cities, on land rented for a cow, with as its basis a compilation of hymns addressed to the gods and goddesses, themselves aspects of nature. This compilation tells the story of its inhabitants, since time immemorial.

---

[1] With Merhgarh.

The 7 Rivers Civilization

The Seven Rivers Civilization was prosperous and seemed to benefit everyone. The absence of war certainly had something to do with it. Different communities lived in harmony, probably speaking different Indo-European languages, as is still the case in this area today. They had Vedic Sanskrit as their language of com munication.
Women were not stigmatized there, and a certain open-mindedness reigned. Unlike other great civilizations, it did not practice slavery and the general impression that results from this is that the people were happy and lived in comfort and material ease, in full agreement with their spirituality.

Of the three great civilizations of the time, it is the least flashy. No monumental buildings, no palaces, no slaves, no armies, no temples, not the slightest trace of violence over a period of at least 1,500 years, no trace of misery. On the other hand, comfort for all, hygiene for all, and simple and happy prosperity for all.

The 7 Rivers Civilization, like all civilizations, eventually stopped. It did not col lapse. Its stoppage was not due to wars or violence, but to climate disruption and two major earthquakes. They diverted the two main tributaries of their sacred river, and even more than sacred since it was one of their goddesses, the only river to have been deified.

But, unlike many other civilizations, it did not disappear. It was transformed. Af ter being forced to move, the inhabitants migrated massively to the Gangetic plain, and, after a few centuries, it gave rise to classical Vedism, which is found in the Mâhabhârata and the Ramâyana and all classical Indian literature.

The real soma having disappeared for a long time. It was replaced by other psychoactive plants, but which were not tryptamines. Nevertheless, the general spirit remained and even developed thanks to the priests who had engaged in the path of the Upanishads. When the veda gave way to the vedanta – the end of the veda, the Indian civilization was gradually transformed to end up, after many invasions, in the modern India that we know.

**Today's world.**

Modern Western civilization has imposed itself on the entire surface of the Earth, mostly by force and corruption.
At the beginning of the 19th century, the United Kingdom shifted its agricultural activity into an activity of mass material production, thanks, essentially, to the plundering of the resources of its colonies, particularly Indian ones. India, which, before the British Râj, was a rich and prosperous country, sank into poverty for the benefit of its colonizer.
France followed, plundering Africa, among other countries, and the whole West rushed into what it thought was an El Dorado, producing consumer goods in large quantities. The effect obtained was to improve material life and to lengthen the quality and life span of Westerners.

Gradually, spirituality disappeared. Monotheistic religions maintained a form of morality, in the service of the powerful, to maintain a certain civilizational coherence. The rise of pure and hard materialism destroyed this morality, which, although very imperfect, maintained a kind of respect for the other, Western of course.

The egos of the dominant, greed and ideologies have generated unprecedented wars, especially in the 20th century which saw two world wars, with the worst horrors imaginable, including the Holocaust and two nuclear bombs.
Of course, man has not become cruel in the last century, but he has industrialized stupidity and cruelty.

Despite a revolt by young Westerners in the 1960s, who did not want this mercantile society at all, the race towards hyper-consumption developed and accelerated brutally from the 1980s. Neo-liberal ideology took power. Greed became a virtue, as did selfishness, brutality, cynicism and vanity.

But, there are no more countries to plunder. We must produce and consume excessively, otherwise the whole thing will collapse. And unlike the 7 Rivers Civilization, it will not happen smoothly.

Experts are unanimous: by dint of producing and consuming, we have almost exhausted all the resources that are essential for us to continue living in this way. The energy that we need in large quantities will no longer be available within a few decades.

By producing and consuming without stopping, we have, in less than two centuries, disrupted the climate and generated a period of natural disasters that is only just beginning.

# The end of civilizations

All civilizations have stopped. Like everything in this Universe, including the Universe itself, they were born, lived and died.
Or almost. In fact, they have transformed or disappeared, leaving archaeologists speechless.

The main causes are:

1. Natural disasters.
2. Environmental degradation.
3. Internal and external wars and conflicts.
4. Economic decline.
5. Instability and corruption.
6. Loss of commercial networks.
7. Epidemics.
8. Special cases.

Of course, several factors combined for most of them.

**Natural disasters.**
Tsunamis, earthquakes, volcanic eruptions, floods, prolonged droughts, general cooling. The list could be endless. As we have seen with regard to the Shushna myth, the great cooling of the northern hemisphere in 6,200 BCE led to a drought that struck North Africa and West Asia. It also generated a sudden rise in sea level and a general cooling that led to population movements towards the equator.

The Minoan civilization was wiped out by a volcanic eruption on the island of Santorini around 1200 BCE, causing a population displacement. On the island, there was up to 40 meters of ash!

The migrations that followed also contributed to the decline of other civilizations in the eastern Mediterranean, adding to other causes.

**Environmental degradation.**

Another important element that can destroy a civilization is the destruction of the environment, which we practice with some fervor. Some of them respected their environment, but others much less.

The Mayans suffered from massive deforestation and soil depletion. Added to some internal conflicts, this caused their downfall.

**Internal and external wars and conflicts.**

There is nothing like a good old war to destroy everything. Internal conflicts are generally due to the betrayal of the elites. When a population organizes itself into a society, the elites, hereditary or not, are responsible for making society function well, in the general interest. But after a certain time, these elites only think of themselves and neglect, or even oppress the rest of the population. Then, inevitably, the rest of the population revolts.

The case of the Roman Empire is well known. It was torn apart by civil wars and was eventually invaded by Germanic peoples.

**The decline of the economy.**

When a civilization is at peace, generally, if the elites do their job well, the econ omy prospers. On the other hand, wars are ruinous, not for everyone[1], of course, but generally the population suffers.

The Western Roman Empire owed its fall largely to an economy weakened by constant military spending and galloping inflation. Of course, the Germanic invasions made the situation worse.

**Political instability and corruption.**

The logical consequence of economic decline is political instability. This is usually accompanied by corruption. When elites forget their role, internal unrest soon appears.

The Han Dynasty in China owes its decline to corruption and internal conflicts.

**Loss of commercial networks.**

---

[1] Arms dealers and manufacturers have no interest in seeing peace reign.

Today, we have a thousand ways to import and export, by sea, by land, and by air. It was less simple a few millennia ago and the breakdown of trade networks could occur relatively easily and wipe out a civilization.
A good example of this is the Late Bronze Age civilizations in the Mediterranean. Following the end of the Minoan civilization, Egypt, and the Hittite empire in particular, collapsed at about the same time.

**Epidemics.**

In 2020, covid 19 is an excellent demonstration that a sudden epidemic can end a civilization quickly. Especially several centuries ago when vaccines did not exist. So, when a plague epidemic occurs, the population is seriously affected.
The Roman Empire was hit by plague epidemics in the 2nd and 6th centuries.

**Special case.**

Mesopotamia: Excessive salinization due to poorly controlled irrigation, combined with invasions and conquests by the Persians and Assyrians, brought down one of the earliest civilizations.

**The Khmer Empire:**

Poor water management, climate change and invasions and wars with neighboring countries weakened civilization until the Siamese invasion,

**Repeated mistakes in human history.**

Concentration of powers and hypercentralization:
Whether it was Egypt, the Roman Empire or the Chinese Empire, power was in the hands of a small and hyper-centralized elite. This concentration of power inevitably leads to abuses of all kinds. Social inequalities that are too obvious lead to revolts. Hyper-centralization often leaves regions far from the capitals abandoned.

Today we see similar trends in some countries, not only Western ones, where excessive concentration of power can lead to corruption and social protest movements.

**Overexploitation of natural resources:**

Civilizations like the Mayans or Easter Island have suffered declines partly due to the overexploitation of their natural resources, leading to famines and social collapses. Today, the overexploitation of natural resources is a catastrophe from which we will have difficulty recovering. It has consequences such as climate change, deforestation, loss of biodiversity, water wars, famines, among others.

**Wars and conflicts:**

History is marked by many conflicts between civilizations, often over territory, resources, or power. The Punic Wars between Rome and Carthage, the Mongol invasions, and many other examples show how wars have often been destructive to civilizations. In our time, wars, which are multiplying, almost everywhere, continue to cause human suffering and massive destruction. We no longer fight in the old way, army against army, but army against everything that lives[1]. Never have so many countries been so armed.
With weapons of a power never seen before in human history, the next world war will be the ultimate in horror.

**Social inequalities and injustices.**

The hoarding of resources by a corrupt elite, the extreme poverty of the weakest everywhere including in the West, the refugees that rich countries let die at their borders, the slavery of the Uighurs in China, apartheid in Israel, the untouchables in post-Vedic India, create a deep feeling of injustice and inequalities that are difficult to bear. Today, although slavery is illegal, social and economic inequalities are still there, aggravated by globalization and economic policies that always serve the same people, the richest. Slavery persists. It has changed its name and is now called wage labor.

**Ignoring warnings:**

Ancient civilizations often ignored early warning signs of their decline. For example, warnings from philosophers and scientists of the time about the dangers

---

[1] See the carnage in Gaza.

of decadence or environmental change were often ignored. Today, similar warnings about climate change, pandemics, or economic crises are completely ignored or downplayed by elites.

Human history is rich in lessons that we continue to ignore, thus repeating the same mistakes. Recognizing these mistakes and learning from history is essential to avoid similar catastrophes in the future. But, for our mercantile civilization, is it not already too late?

\*\*\*

The future of our globalized mercantile and materialistic civilization is therefore rather bleak. Unless our elites become aware of this extremely quickly, we are heading straight for a wall.

Oh, of course, at the last moment, those who have not left[1] with the cash register, will try to react. But it will be too late. Much too late.

These are the effects of karma. This word means action, deed. The law of karma is that every action or deed has one or more consequences. These consequences are both internal and external. When we base our entire lives on non-renewable resources, it is no wonder that when they are exhausted we will no longer be able to live.

In a few centuries, we have destroyed biodiversity, ravaged our natural environment, built and stockpiled quantities of weapons more destructive than anything invented since the beginning of humanity. We have built civilizations based on competition, on frenzied individualism, on greed, on hatred of others, on hypocrisy and the absence of the most basic humanist morality...

Westerners no longer rule the planet, and that is a good thing. They have committed the worst crimes against the peoples they colonized. The most serious of all these crimes are not the massacres, rapes and pillaging[2], but the humiliation and dehumanization of the conquered peoples. We will have to pay the bill one day or another.

---

[1] On Mars?
[2] In the name of God or human rights.

The elites have betrayed. But, with rare exceptions, the elites always betray. They have other things to do than really take care of the well-being of their fellow citizens. They have to satisfy their ego: get re-elected, in what are called democracies, and leave their names in History. In dictatorships, you have to keep power by all means, in the greatest paranoia, because dictators end badly. Whatever the political system, those who are rich, and therefore who have power or who want to be as close to it as possible, betray. And those who suffer are always the same.

Wars are multiplying and will multiply even more. Let's take a European country that calls itself the country of human rights, the country of Lights and whose motto is: liberty, equality, fraternity. It is the second largest arms seller in the world! Just behind the USA!
So when his voice calls for peace and negotiation, how can we believe it? Its interest is to sell weapons, everywhere, to all countries! And of course, these weapons are used, because its factories have to run. The good health of the GDP depends on it.
No matter what country we live in, we are in a spiral from which we cannot escape. We would have to stop everything immediately, and that is totally impossible.

In a few decades, we will no longer be able to live on this planet, because of the heat, the lack of water, the exhaustion of our resources, wars, epidemics from hot countries... The list is too long, unfortunately.

## So, is it over?

Well, maybe not. Some paradigms are shifting. If the overwhelming majority of the world's population continues to think we're headed in the right direction, not everyone does.

There is, fortunately, a minority that intends to put an end to the current way of thinking and acting. Solidarity networks are springing up everywhere. These net works have no leaders. They do not have Great Men at their head. They are simple and human people. We are only at the beginning, they will grow and multiply in the face of the advance of the final catastrophe. They are the ones who will save us, if it is still possible, and not the politicians, the armies, or the multi-billionaires.

Another positive point has emerged in less than ten years: the de-demonization of psychedelics.
When they were banned by Richard Nixon and the American Christian fundamentalist sects, they were classified as one of the most dangerous drugs in the world, on a par with heroin and alcohol!!!
But recently, doctors and researchers have resumed their analyses[1], and have found that these products are neither addictive nor dangerous to health. When used properly, they cure the ills of our time: depression, malaise and addictions, in a single session, or two for the most difficult cases.
When they are misused, the worst that can happen is to spend a few very unpleasant hours, But that's it. There are no after-effects, except for people who are already psychotic[2].
But as we have seen above, these psychedelics dissolve the ego by introducing the one who takes them to a great spiritual adventure that changes his life.
The 7 Rivers Civilization used them and existed, for at least 1,500 years, without war, without violence and in the interest of all.

However, a huge drought put an end to this practical and effective spiritual practice, so there is no ideal solution.
But if we can learn from the past, perhaps we can rebuild a civilization, after its final collapse, that is humane, united and fraternal?

The next few years will clearly tell us whether we are heading towards a Mad Max 2 scenario, only much worse, or whether we are going to seriously change our society to make it something that is humane and fraternal.

Gwell'vo[3] as we say in Brittany

---

[1] In countries where research is free.
[2] And who can be treated by........ psychedelics.
[3] We 'll see.

The 7 Rivers Civilization

# Bibliography

The Veda:

Keith, A. Berriedale. The Religion and Philosophy of the Veda and Upanishads. Cambridge: Harvard University Press, 1925.
Gonda, Jan. Vedic Literature (Saṃhitās and Brāhmaṇas). Wiesbaden: Otto Harrassowitz, 1975.
Staal, Frits. Discovering the Vedas: Origins, Mantras, Rituals, Insights. New Delhi: Penguin India, 2008.
Macdonell, Arthur Anthony. A History of Sanskrit Literature. London: Longmans, Green, and Co., 1900.
Witzel, Michael. The Vedas: Texts, Language & Ritual. Delhi: Motilal Banarsidass, 2003.
Holdrege, Barbara A. Veda and Torah: Transcending the Textuality of Scripture. Albany: State University of New York Press, 1996.
Basham, A.L. The Wonder That Was India. New York: Grove Press, 1954.
Gonda, Jan. Aspects of Early Vedism. Delhi: Motilal Banarsidass, 1963.
Haug, Martin. The Aitareya Brahmanam of the Rigveda: The First English Translation with Commentary. London: Trübner & Co., 1863.
Renou, Louis. Vedic India. Calcutta: Susil Gupta (India) Ltd., 1957.
Patton, Laurie L. Bringing the Gods to Mind: Mantra and Ritual in Early Indian Sacrifice. Berkeley: University of California Press, 2005.
Kaelber, Walter O. Tapta Marga: Asceticism and Initiation in Vedic India. Albany: State University of New York Press, 1989.

The Rig Veda

Jamison, Stephanie W. and Joel P. Brereton. The Rigveda: The Earliest Religious Poetry of India. Oxford: Oxford University Press, 2014.
Griffith, Ralph T.H. The Hymns of the Rigveda. London: Trübner & Co., 1889.
Doniger, Wendy. The Rig Veda: An Anthology. New York: Penguin Books, 1981.
O'Flaherty, Wendy Doniger. The Rig Veda. New York: Viking Press, 1981.
Haug, Martin. The Aitareya Brahmanam of the Rigveda. London: Trübner & Co., 1863.
Macdonell, Arthur Anthony. Vedic Mythology. Strassburg: Trübner, 1897.
Renou, Louis. The Nature of the Rig Veda. Calcutta: Susil Gupta, 1957.
Gonda, Jan. Aspects of Early Vedism. Delhi: Motilal Banarsidass, 1963.
Elizarenkova, Tatyana. Language and Style of the Vedic Ṛṣis. Albany: State University of New York Press, 1995.
Witzel, Michael. Inside the Texts, Beyond the Texts: New Approaches to the Study of the Vedas. Cambridge: Harvard University Press, 1997.
Staal, Frits. The Science of Ritual in the Rig Veda. Delhi: Motilal Banarsidass, 1986.
Gonda, Jan. Vedic Ritual: The Rigveda Samhita. Leiden: Brill, 1960.

Patton, Laurie L. Bringing the Gods to Mind: Mantra and Ritual in Early Indian Sacrifice. Berkeley: University of California Press, 2005.
Muir, John. Original Sanskrit Texts on the Origin and History of the People of India, Their Religion and Institutions. London: Trübner, 1868.
Saraswati, Dayananda. Rig Veda Bhashya. Bombay: Arya Pratinidhi Sabha, 1877.

The Spiritual and Healing Use of Psychedelics

Grof, Stanislav. The Holotropic Mind: The Three Levels of Human Consciousness and How They Shape Our Lives. New York: HarperCollins, 1992.
Leary, Timothy. The Psychedelic Experience: A Manual Based on the Tibetan Book of the Dead. New York: Citadel Press, 1964.
Grof, Stanislav. LSD Psychotherapy: The Healing Potential of Psychedelic Medicine. Santa Cruz: MAPS, 1980.
Strassman, Rick. DMT: The Spirit Molecule. Rochester: Park Street Press, 2001.
McKenna, Terence. Food of the Gods: The Search for the Original Tree of Knowledge. New York: Bantam Books, 1992.
Pinchbeck, Daniel. Breaking Open the Head: A Psychedelic Journey into the Heart of Contemporary Shamanism. New York: Broadway Books, 2002.
Pollan, Michael. How to Change Your Mind: What the New Science of Psychedelics Teaches Us About Consciousness, Dying, Addiction, Depression, and Transcendence. New York: Penguin Press, 2018.
Shulgin, Alexander, and Ann Shulgin. PiHKAL: A Chemical Love Story. Berkeley: Transform Press, 1991.
Weil, Andrew. The Natural Mind: An Investigation of Drugs and the Higher Consciousness. Boston: Houghton Mifflin, 1972.
Metzner, Ralph. The Ayahuasca Experience: A Sourcebook on the Sacred Vine of Spirits. Rochester: Park Street Press, 1999.

The civilizations of Oxus, Oases and ancient Iran

Francfort, Henri-Paul. The Archaeology of the Oxus Civilization. Cambridge: Cambridge University Press, 2019.
Masson, Vadim M., and Victor H. Sarianidi. Central Asia: Turkmenistan. Geneva: Nagel Publishers, 1977.
Potts, Daniel T. The Archaeology of Elam: Formation and Transformation of an Ancient Iranian State. Cambridge: Cambridge University Press, 1999.
Kohl, Philip L. The Bronze Age Civilization of Central Asia: Recent Soviet Discoveries. New York: Sharpe, 1981.
Hiebert, Fredrik Talmage. The Ancient Oasis Civilizations of Central Asia. Oxford: Oxford University Press, 1994.
Sarianidi, Viktor. Margiana and Protozoroastrianism. Naples: Instituto Universitario Orientale, 1998.

Ligabue, Giancarlo, and Svetlana Pankova. Oxus: Treasures of Central Asia. Venice: Ligabue Study and Research Centre, 2012.
Ghirshman, Roman. Iran: From the Earliest Times to the Islamic Conquest. Harmondsworth: Penguin Books, 1954.
Kohl, Philip L., and C.C. Lamberg-Karlovsky. The Bronze Age Civilization of Central Asia. Cambridge: Cambridge University Press, 1981.
Cerasetti, Barbara. The Oasis Civilizations of Central Asia. Berlin: de Gruyter, 2020.

## Current global warming

Hansen, James. Storms of My Grandchildren: The Truth About the Coming Climate Catastrophe and Our Last Chance to Save Humanity. New York: Bloomsbury, 2009.
Mann, Michael E. The New Climate War: The Fight to Take Back Our Planet. New York: PublicAffairs, 2021.
Klein, Naomi. This Changes Everything: Capitalism vs. the Climate. New York: Simon & Schuster, 2014.
Lenton, Timothy M. Earth System Science: A Very Short Introduction. Oxford: Oxford University Press, 2016.
Kolbert, Elizabeth. The Sixth Extinction: An Unnatural History. New York: Henry Holt, 2014.
Wallace-Wells, David. The Uninhabitable Earth: Life After Warming. New York: Tim Duggan Books, 2019.
Flannery, Tim. The Weather Makers: How Man Is Changing the Climate and What It Means for Life on Earth. New York: Grove Press, 2005.
Steffen, Will, et al. The Anthropocene: Conceptual and Historical Perspectives. Cambridge: Cambridge University Press, 2011.
Koonin, Steven E. Unsettled: What Climate Science Tells Us, What It Doesn't, and Why It Matters. Dallas: BenBella Books, 2021.
Monbiot, George. Heat: How to Stop the Planet Burning. New York: Doubleday, 2006.

## The destruction of biodiversity

Wilson, Edward O. The Diversity of Life. Cambridge: Harvard University Press, 1992.
Kolbert, Elizabeth. The Sixth Extinction: An Unnatural History. New York: Henry Holt, 2014.
Quammen, David. The Song of the Dodo: Island Biogeography in an Age of Extinctions. New York: Scribner, 1996.
Cafaro, Philip, and Eileen Crist. Life on the Brink: Environmentalists Confront Overpopulation. Athens: University of Georgia Press, 2012.
Chivian, Eric, and Aaron Bernstein. Sustaining Life: How Human Health Depends on Biodiversity. Oxford: Oxford University Press, 2008.
Leakey, Richard, and Roger Lewin. The Sixth Extinction: Patterns of Life and the Future of Humankind. New York: Doubleday, 1995.
Pimm, Stuart L. The World According to Pimm: A Scientist Audits the Earth. New York: McGraw-Hill, 2001.

Dirzo, Rodolfo, et al. Biodiversity and Ecosystem Services: The View from the Americas. Washington D.C.: Island Press, 2005.
Sodhi, Navjot S., and Paul R. Ehrlich. Conservation Biology for All. Oxford: Oxford University Press, 2010.
Stork, Nigel E. Biodiversity: An Introduction. Cambridge: Cambridge University Press, 1995.

The Future Prospects of Humanity

Diamond, Jared. Collapse: How Societies Choose to Fail or Succeed. New York: Viking, 2005.
Harari, Yuval Noah. Homo Deus: A Brief History of Tomorrow. New York: Harper, 2016.
Schwab, Klaus. The Fourth Industrial Revolution. New York: Crown Business, 2017.
Bostrom, Nick. Superintelligence: Paths, Dangers, Strategies. Oxford: Oxford University Press, 2014.
Steffen, Will, et al. The Anthropocene: Conceptual and Historical Perspectives. Cambridge: Cambridge University Press, 2011.
Attali, Jacques. A Brief History of the Future: A Brave and Controversial Look at the Twenty-First Century. New York: Arcade Publishing, 2011.
Schneider, Francois. The Future of Our Global Energy Supply: With A New Approach to Energy Management and Transfer. New York: Springer, 2014.
Servigne, Pablo, et Raphaël Stevens. How Everything Can Collapse: A Manual for Our Times. Cambridge: Polity Press, 2020.
Kurzweil, Ray. The Singularity Is Near: When Humans Transcend Biology. New York: Viking, 2005.
Schneider-Mayerson, Matthew. Peak Oil: Apocalyptic Environmentalism and Libertarian Political Culture. Chicago: University of Chicago Press, 2015.

# The 7 Rivers Civilization

https://rigveda.blog

# The 7 Rivers Civilization